General Prisons Board

General Prisons Board Ireland

Twenty-first report, 1898-99, with appendix

General Prisons Board

General Prisons Board Ireland
Twenty-first report, 1898-99, with appendix

ISBN/EAN: 9783742805584

Manufactured in Europe, USA, Canada, Australia, Japa

Cover: Foto ©Lupo / pixelio.de

Manufactured and distributed by brebook publishing software
(www.brebook.com)

General Prisons Board

General Prisons Board Ireland

TWENTY-FIRST REPORT

OF THE

GENERAL PRISONS BOARD, IRELAND,

1898-99;

WITH AN APPENDIX.

Presented to both Houses of Parliament by Command of Her Majesty.

DUBLIN:
PRINTED FOR HER MAJESTY'S STATIONERY OFFICE,
BY ALEXANDER THOM & CO. (LIMITED).

And to be purchased, either directly or through any Bookseller, from
HODGES, FIGGIS, & CO. (LIMITED), 104, GRAFTON-STREET, DUBLIN; or
EYRE & SPOTTISWOODE, EAST HARDING-STREET, FLEET-STREET, E.C., and
32, ABINGDON-STREET, WESTMINSTER, S.W.; or
JOHN MENZIES & CO., 12, HANOVER-STREET, EDINBURGH, and
90, WEST NILE-STREET, GLASGOW.

1899.

[C.—9439.] Price 6½d.

SIR,

I have to acknowledge the receipt of your letter of the 10th instant, forwarding, for submission to His Excellency the Lord Lieutenant, the Twenty-first Annual Report of the General Prisons Board for Ireland.

I am,

Sir,

Your obedient servant,

D. HARREL.

The Chairman.
General Prisons Board,
Dublin Castle.

CONTENTS.

TWENTY-FIRST REPORT

OF THE

GENERAL PRISONS BOARD, IRELAND.

TO HIS EXCELLENCY GEORGE HENRY,
EARL CADOGAN, K.G.,

LORD LIEUTENANT-GENERAL AND GENERAL GOVERNOR OF IRELAND.

General Prisons Board,
Dublin Castle,
14th July, 1899.

MAY IT PLEASE YOUR EXCELLENCY,

We have the honour, pursuant to statute, to present this our Twenty-first Annual Report on the condition of the prisons and prisoners within our jurisdiction, and with respect to the registration of criminals.

The number of prisons and bridewells remains the same as at the date of our last report, namely :— *Number of prisons.*

1 Prison for male convicts only (Maryborough).
1 Prison for male convicts and local prisoners (Mountjoy, Dublin).
1 Prison for female convicts and local prisoners (Mountjoy.)
10 Prisons for male and female local prisoners.
6 Prisons for male local prisoners only.
2 Prisons for female local prisoners only.
6 Minor Prisons and 1 District Bridewell for male and female prisoners on remand, or under sentences not exceeding seven days.
13 Bridewells for male and female prisoners on remand, or under sentences not exceeding three days.

The lock-up which was opened at Ennis, in 1867, in the building formerly used as the County Clare Prison, was closed during the past year—namely, on the 1st March, 1899. The building

State Inebriate Reformatory. has since been converted into a State Inebriate Reformatory for Criminal Drunkards, committed under the Inebriates Act, 1898, Section 1 of that Act provides that :—

1.—(1.) Where a person is convicted on indictment of an offence punishable with imprisonment or penal servitude, if the Court is satisfied from the evidence that the offence was committed under the influence of drink or that drunkenness was a contributing cause of the offence, and the offender admits that he is or is found by the jury to be a habitual drunkard, the Court may, in addition to or in substitution for any other sentence, order that he be detained for a term not exceeding three years in any State inebriate reformatory, or in any certified inebriate reformatory the managers of which are willing to receive him.

(2.) In any indictment under this section it shall be sufficient, after charging the offence, to state that the offender is a habitual drunkard. In the proceedings on the indictment the offender shall, in the first instance, be arraigned on so much only of the indictment as charges the said offence, and, if on arraignment he pleads guilty or is found guilty by the jury, the jury shall, unless the offender admits that he is a habitual drunkard, be charged to inquire whether he is a habitual drunkard, and in that case it shall not be necessary to swear the jury again.

Provided that, unless evidence that the offender is a habitual drunkard has been given before he is committed for trial, not less than seven days' notice shall be given to the proper officer of the Court by which the offender is to be tried, and to the offender that it is intended to charge habitual drunkenness in the indictment.

At present there are no inebriates in custody.

The regulations for the reformatory, having been duly laid before Parliament, came into effect on the 1st June, 1899. A copy of these regulations will be found in the Appendix.

Enlargement of Maryborough Convict Prison. In our last Annual Report we mentioned that a scheme had been approved for the enlargement of Maryborough Convict Prison by the addition of a new block to accommodate 200 male convicts.

A contract has been entered into for the erection of this block, and the work is now in progress. When it is completed it is intended to transfer all the male convicts, except those undergoing the earlier months of their sentences in separate confinement, from Mountjoy to Maryborough Prison, which will then contain over 300 cells, with a farm of 34 acres, and will thus become the principal male convict prison in Ireland.

Accommodation. In Table XIX. of the Appendix, a return is given of the accommodation in the convict and the several larger local prisons.

Number of local prisoners. We subjoin a table of committals to local prisons, and daily average number of local prisoners during a series of years.

COMMITTALS, &c., exclusive of Prisoners Committed under Civil Process.

Year.	Number of Committals	Daily Average No. of Prisoners.	Proportion of that Average on each 1000 of estimated population.
1854, ...	60,445	5,740	63
1855, ...	48,446	4,418	73
1856, ...	30,712	2,553	42
1870, ...	33,370	2,227	41
1879-80, . . .	44,659	2,617	38
1888-90, . . .	39,792	2,346	43
1890-91, . . .	40,153	2,605	55
1891-92, . . .	37,366	2,497	53
1892-93, . . .	34,583	8,815	50
1893-94, . . .	34,267	2,416	53
1894-95, . . .	31,474	2,317	50
1895, ...	30,370	2,155	47
1896, ...	53,956	1,725	51
1897, ...	34,911	2,333	51
1898, ...	36,113	2,563	56

From this Table it will be seen that there has been an increase of 3,202 committals as compared with 1807, the number for that year having been about the average for the nine years ending with 1897.

From a comparison of the committals, prison by prison, it appears that in the rural districts the numbers remain about the same, and that the increase is almost entirely in the prisons of the three principal cities—Dublin, Belfast, and Cork.

The following figures show both the increase in the prisons named, and the nearly stationary condition of the numbers in the other prisons in 1808, as compared with 1897:—

—	Dublin.	Belfast.	Cork.	All other Prisons.
1898, .	13,803	7,329	3,449	13,492
1897, .	11,934	6,682	3,042	13,263
Increase, .	1,879	647	417	229

Further investigation shows that the number of drunkards committed has risen from 16,208 in 1807, to 17,807 in 1808, being in each year about 47 per cent., or nearly one-half of the total committals. This cause alone therefore accounts for an increase of 1,500, or nearly one-half of the total increase during the past year. The proportion of prisoners committed for drunkenness to the number of *convicted* prisoners is considerably greater, having for the past two years been about 59 per cent.

Committals to bridewells are not included in the table above. Bridewells. The numbers of such committals during 1898 were 963 males and 237 females, the numbers for the previous year having been 1,023 males and 204 females.

As means of communication by rail increase, and as it is better understood how unsuitable bridewells are for any but the shortest periods of detention, the committals to them are steadily declining.

The following table shows the number of convicts at various periods during past years. Those in the first column are included in the table of committals given above, all convicts being in the first instance committed to local prisons :—

Year.	No. Convicted.	No. Discharged.*	In custody on January 1st.		
	M. and F.	M. and F.	M.	F.	Total.
1854	710	658	—	—	(2,033
1855	318	630	3,097	330	3,427
1860	331	524	1,187	444	1,631
1870	245	253	878	354	1,230
1879–80	134	291	819	212	1,031
1889–90	83	104	426	28	454
1890–91	68	110	425	38	463
1891–92	105	117	443	37	480
1892–93	96	113	441	30	471
1893–94	106	103	446	39	485
1894–95	115	157	427	37	464
1895	104	134	417	37	454
1896	81	140	399	30	429
1897	65	114	360	37	397
1898	91	138	311	31	343

* Including those re-discharged after forfeiture or revocation of licence.
In addition to this number there were 245 convicts under detention in the county prisons, and several hundreds in Bermuda and Gibraltar, who were subsequently discharged in Ireland.

The number of convicts convicted during the year shows an increase on the previous year, but owing to the practice of inflicting shorter sentences since the passing of the Penal Servitude Act of 1891, which reduced the minimum term of penal servitude from 5 to 3 years, the convicts in custody are still decreasing, and at present number only 300 males and 10 females. Of 91 sentenced during the year, 51 were sentenced to the shortest term —3 years.

Particulars of the length of the sentences are given in table below :—

	Males	Females	Total
3 years,	47	4	51
5 „	6	—	6
6 „	15	7	17
7 „	5	—	5
10 „	7	—	7
20 „	1	—	1
Life,	1	—	1
Death (commuted to P. S. for life)	3	—	3
Gross total sentenced during year.	85	6	91

The nature of the discharges of convicts during the year was
as follows:—

	Males.	Females.	Total.
On Commutation of Sentence,	2	1	3
On Licence,	116	19	135
Total,	118	20	138

The Revocations and Forfeitures of Licences in Ireland
during the year ended 31st December, 1898, were as follow:—

	Males.	Females.	Total.
Forfeited for breach of conditions of Licence,	16	—	16
Forfeited or revoked in consequence of a conviction for other offences,	21	4	25
Gross Total,	37	4	41

Particulars of the punishments inflicted during the year 1898
will be found in Table XIV. of the Appendix, where the total
number of local prisoners punished is shown to be 2,685, and of
convicts 105. After deducting prisoners transferred, and thus
appearing twice in the returns, the number of local prisoners
punished represents a percentage of 6·5 and the number of
convicts punished a percentage of 23·5 on the total number of
local prisoners and convicts respectively in custody during the
year.

The total number of juvenile convicted prisoners during
1898 has been practically the same as in 1897. The number
under 12 years of age, however, has decreased from 36 to 19.

Years.	Under 12 Years of age		12 to 16 Years of age		Total.		
	Boys.	Girls.	Boys.	Girls.	Boys.	Girls.	Boys & Girls
1889-90,	63	1	330	69	393	70	163
1890-91,	44	8	337	63	381	71	452
1891-92,	53	—	344	63	397	63	462
1892-93,	29	1	305	72	334	73	409
1893-94,	37	4	250	61	287	65	372
1894-95,	15	8	318	56	243	59	302
1895,	20	—	207	60	227	30	257
1896,	15	5	172	17	187	20	207
1897,	35	1	170	15	205	16	221
1898,	19	—	180	23	199	23	222

The figures above refer only to convicted juveniles. Besides
these 11 boys and 1 girl under 12 years of age, and 67 boys and
13 girls from 12 to 16 years, were committed to prison during
1898, but were subsequently either acquitted, or discharged on
various grounds (no prosecution, &c.), with the exception of four
who were awaiting trial at the end of the year.

PARTICULARS of the 19 CONVICTED MALE JUVENILES, under 12 years
of age, COMMITTED to PRISON during the year 1898 :—

Prison.	Initials of Name.	Age (Years).	Offence.	Sentence.
Armagh, .	J. M'K.	10	Larceny of 1d., . . .	14 days' hard labour, and 7 years' Reformatory.
Belfast, . .	J. W.	10¼	I. Throwing stones, .	I. 7 days or }to follow. 14s. 10d.
			II. Assault. . . .	II. 1 day, or } 11s. 6d.
	G. R.	10	Larceny, ...	5 years in Industrial School.*
Clonmel, .	R. R.	11	Maliciously place stones on railway line.	1 calendar month Imprisonment, without hard labour.
	E. R.	9	Steal ass and cart. .	14 days' Imprisonment and 5 years' in Reformatory.
Cork Male, .	J. S.	10	Trespass, ...	7 days or 1s.
	F. M.	11	Housebreaking, . .	Bound to keep the peace.
	W. K.	11	Housebreaking, . .	Do. do.
Kilmainham, .	J. R.	8½	Stealing a box of figs, value 4s. 6d.	5 years Reformatory.]
Mountjoy, .	J. D.	10	Stealing the arm of life from his father.	14 days Imprisonment and 5 years Reformatory.
	J. D.	10	Maliciously broke gas lamps.	14 days Imprisonment and 5 years Reformatory.
	M. D.	10	Stealing 9 pairs of boots,	14 days Imprisonment and 5 years Reformatory.
	P. R.	11	Stealing a mouth organ, value 6d.	14 days Imprisonment and 5 years Reformatory.
	J. R.	11	Stealing a hand-cart and newspapers, value £1 5s.	14 days Imprisonment and 5 years Reformatory.
	J. D.	11	Begging on public thoroughfare.	14 days Imprisonment and 5 years Reformatory.
	J. P.	11	Wilfully broke glass, value 6d.	7 days or bail.
	J. C.	10	Found in dwelling-house for unlawful purpose.	14 days Imprisonment and 5 years Reformatory.
Tralee, . .	W. C.	11	Feloniously break and enter a dwelling-house and steal therefrom 1d.	14 days and 5 years Reformatory.
	J. S.	11	Begging and gathering alms.	One week's Imprisonment.

* Sent direct from Court to School after Conviction.
† . . . Reformatory .

Under the special rules for juvenile offenders, which were
adopted in 1898, all juveniles under 16 years of age are specially
treated. If their sentences amount to one month or upwards,
they are removed to Mountjoy Prison, Dublin, where accommodation
is set apart for them. The number so removed during 1898
was 20. The shorter sentences are undergone in the prisons
to which the juveniles are first committed. In all prisons special
means are adopted to keep them from coming in contact with
adult prisoners, and special attention is devoted to them by the
Governors and Chaplains. They are provided with special library
books and a larger amount of employment in the open air than
older prisoners, and receive physical drill.

The health of the prisoners was on the whole satisfactory.

Subjoined is a table of mortality among local prisoners and convicts for each year during the last ten years:—

	LOCAL PRISONERS			CONVICTS		
YEAR.	Daily Average Number of Prisoners.	No. of Deaths.	Rate per Thousand.	Daily Average Number of Prisoners.	No. of Deaths.	Rate per Thousand.
1849-80.	3,148	11	5·5	421	7	17
1880-1.	2,410	3	1·15	449	7	63
1881-9.	7,460	9	5·6	172	8	17
1882-3.	2,791	11	171	470	4	80
1883-4.	2,458	13	5·23	180	3	67
1884-5.	1,125	4	154	460	3	17
1885.	1,104	2	179	151	3	11·4
1886.	1,245	6	5·16	153	1	25
1887.	7,348	7	2·99	331	3	1·4
1888.	7,474	10	3·65	840	6	14·8

Of the 10 deaths of local prisoners pneumonia caused two, and asthma, heart disease, and chronic affection of the liver each caused one. Two resulted from exhaustion after excessive drinking, one from sudden cardiac failure, and two were cases of suicide. Of the five convicts who died, one death arose from Bright's disease, one from spinal paralysis, one from pneumonia, one from intestinal tuberculosis, and one from acute peritonitis. There was a considerable number of cases of influenza, but not of a severe type. Otherwise the amount of zymotic disease was slight. There were two cases of typhus fever; in one of these the fever was incubating when the prisoner was admitted; in the other instance also it was probably brought in by the prisoner, but this point could not be established with certainty. Of enteric fever likewise there were two cases, one of which was developing at the time of admission. Although for a considerable part of the year typhoid fever prevailed to an excessive degree throughout the City of Belfast, no case of that disease arose in the prison.

On medical grounds 45 local prisoners and 2 convicts were discharged before their sentence had expired. Of these 17 were women very near their confinement, while of the remaining 28 the diseases in 21 cases originated before reception.

There were 70 cases of insanity amongst local prisoners and 5 amongst convicts. Of the 70 local prisoners there were 55 insane at the time of committal; 6 were described as weak-minded or erratic; and 2 as imbecile; 16 were sane. Of the 10 who were sane, 2 had been ordered to be detained during the pleasure of the Lord Lieutenant as having been insane at the time of committing the offence, but were sane during their detention in prison; 2 were epileptics; 1 was a case of recurrent mania who had been previously in an asylum, and 1 when a month in prison developed general paralysis of the insane.

Education.

From Table IX. it will be seen that of 544 male and female local prisoners who were classed on committal as "wholly ignorant," 97 learned to read, write, and calculate, 90 to read and write, and 173 to read. Arrangements were made during the year whereby schoolmaster warders devote more time to the education of illiterate prisoners than was formerly the case.

Visiting Committees of local prisons.

A Return, similar to that published in previous years, showing the number of visits paid to the several prisons by members of the Visiting Committees during the year 1898, is subjoined.

Prisons.	Number of Meetings at which a quorum was present	Number of Visits paid by individual Members.	Prisons.	Number of Meetings at which a quorum was present.	Number of Visits paid by individual Members.
LARGER PRISONS.			**LARGER PRISONS—**continued.		
Armagh, . . .	6	71	Sligo, . . .	11	3
Belfast, . . .	1	4	Tralee, . . .	5	7
Castlebar, . . .	5	2	Tullamore, . . .	8	9
Clonmel, . . .	9	18	Waterford, . . .	5	72
Cork, Male, . . .	10	53	Wexford, . . .	11	3
Cork, Female, . . .	5				
Dundalk, . . .	9	9			
Galway, . . .		4	**MINOR PRISONS.**		
Kilkenny, . . .	1	7			
Kilmainham, . . .	6	18	Carrick-on-Shannon,	-	15
Limerick, Male, . . .	5	8	Drogheda, . . .	-	-
Limerick, Female, . . .	5	21	Enniskillen, . . .	-	7
Londonderry, . . .	7	4	Mullingar, . . .	-	1
Mountjoy, . . .	12	10	Omagh, . . .	1	1
Mountjoy, Female, . . .	11	9	Wicklow, . . .	1	4

The Board have to report that during the last year, as during previous years, valuable public services have been rendered by the Visiting Committees generally in the inspection of prisons and the maintenance of discipline amongst prisoners.

Visitors of Convict prisons

The same visitors as in the previous year were last year appointed by Your Excellency to visit the Convict prisons, and visited these institutions as follows:—

	Date of Visits.	No. of Visitors.
Mountjoy Prison, . . .	7 : 4 : 98	5
	6 : 12 : 98	3
Maryborough Prison, . . .	19 : 1 : 98	1
	9 : 2 : 98	1
	16 : 2 : 98	1
	9 : 3 : 98	2
	13 : 4 : 98	1
	11 : 5 : 98	2
	8 : 6 : 98	2
	13 : 7 : 98	2
	10 : 8 : 98	1
	14 : 9 : 98	1
	18 : 10 : 98	2
	14 : 12 : 98	1

Prison Industries.

The Board beg to refer to their last and previous annual Reports for the details of the industries carried on in prisons; also to Table No XXIV. in the Appendix to this Report.

It is observed that prisoners take as much interest in the gardening and farm work as if the crops were their own.

Weaving is a specially useful and interesting industry.

The profit on the Manufacturing Department for the year was £1,371 18s., being an increase of £63 7s. 9d. over the previous year.

In order to stimulate those prison officers who, though not holding appointments as Trade Wardens, instruct and supervise prisoners in certain industries, the Board are glad to report that, with the approval of the Treasury, a number of special allowances of £10 and £5 each, per annum, will be distributed amongst those officers in future.

In former times in selecting prisoners to act as cooks, cleaners, &c., and on other "fatigue" duties, it was the practice to select those longest in prison, if well-conducted, irrespective of the question whether such prisoners were habitual criminals or not.

This practice has been altered, and now such employments are confined to first offenders, so that old offenders who have failed to reform may not be afforded an opportunity of contaminating others, and may receive no exceptional indulgence.

All larger prisons are kept in good repair and condition. The minor prisons are old county prisons only partially occupied. Such portions as are occupied are in good condition.

The new hospital at Belfast Prison, to which reference was made in the last Report, has been completed, and forms a valuable addition to the prison.

In Tables XXVII. and XXVIII. will be found particulars of the expenditure on prisons during the past and several previous years.

The law in regard to prisoners committed to prison in Ireland in default of payment of a fine has been amended by the Fine or Imprisonment (Scotland and Ireland) Act, which has been lately passed.

The object of the measure is stated in the explanatory memorandum accompanying the Bill as follows:—

> Up to January 1st, 1899, a prisoner committed to prison in default of payment of a fine, whether in England and Wales, Scotland, or Ireland, could only obtain release before the expiration of the period for which he was committed by payment of the full amount of the fine. The Departmental Committee of 1894 on Habitual Offenders, &c. (Scotland), strongly recommended that prisoners so committed should be allowed to work out their sentences partly by imprisonment and partly by money payments—a remission of their term of imprisonment in default being made, proportionate to the part of the fine imposed which they were able and willing to pay,—in other words, that a prisoner who had been sentenced, say, to a fine of twenty shillings or twenty days, and who could raise, say, ten shillings, should be liberated after ten days' imprisonment on payment of that ten shillings, instead of being kept in gaol till the very end unless he could pay the entire sum. This recommendation was adopted in the Prison Act, 1898, which came into effect on the first day of the present year. That Act, however, does not apply to Scotland or Ireland, and the object of this Bill is to extend to these countries the same reform in that respect which that measure enacted for England. The enacting clause of the Bill follows verbatim the wording of the Prison Act.

14   *Twenty-first Report, &c.*

Prisoners' Aid Societies. The following are the existing certified Prisoners Aid Societies:—

DUBLIN:

Roman Catholic Female Prisoners' Aid Society.
Roman Catholic Male Prisoners' Aid Society.
Society for the Relief of Poor Protestants (Male and Female) discharged from Prison.

BELFAST:

Prison Gate Mission for Women (Protestant).
Prison Gate Mission for Men (Protestant).
Male Catholic Discharged Prisoners' Aid Society.

LIMERICK:

Limerick Prisoners' Aid Society (undenominational).

CORK:

Female Roman Catholic Prisoners' Aid Society.

These societies render valuable assistance, and it is to be regretted that there is not a society in connection with every prison.

Registration of Criminals. It will be seen from Table XXVI. in the Appendix that the number of discharged convicts and habitual criminals registered in the year 1898 was 150, as compared with 174 in the previous year.

The usual lists of habitual criminals released during the year have been printed and distributed amongst the police.

Anthropometric measurements with finger prints and photographs were taken in the cases of 101 male convicts, and 17 habitual criminals.

Departmental. Captain A. B. C. S. Hill, who was appointed Inspector of Prisons in 1878, retired on Superannuation in September last. Mr. W. V. Harrel was in the same month appointed by Your Excellency to succeed him.

Appendix. We beg to refer to the Appendix for copies of various circulars issued during the year, extracts from reports of superior officers of Convict prisons, and tabular returns.

We have the honour to be,

Your Excellency's obedient servants,

J. S. GIBBONS, *Chairman.*
JOHN MULHALL, *Vice-Chairman.*
STEWART WOODHOUSE.

APPENDIX

TO

TWENTY-FIRST REPORT OF THE GENERAL PRISONS BOARD.

PART I.

CIRCULARS AND CIRCULAR MEMORANDA.

General Prisons Board, Dublin Castle,
18th June, 1898.

To the Governors (or other officers in charge) of H.M. Prisons.

Insanity.

I am to instruct you that if any prisoner committed for Contempt of Court should become insane, in addition to forwarding the usual certificate of insanity to this Office, you should report the fact direct to the Court, under whose order such prisoner is confined, in the same manner as if the case were one where the prisoner's life is considered by the Medical Officer to be endangered by confinement. See Circular 76 (3,451).

By order,
S. H. DOUGLAS,
Secretary.

General Prisons Board, Dublin Castle,
6th December, 1898.

Hard Labour.

To the Governors (or other officers in charge) of H.M. Female Prisons.

Until further orders, washing, in separate compartments, duly tasked in case of prisoners sentenced to hard labour, is approved by the Board as labour at which female prisoners in Probation Class may be employed.

This approval does not extend to the ironing or making up of clothes (11,077).

By order,
S. H. DOUGLAS,
Secretary.

General Prisons Board, Dublin Castle,
6th January, 1899.

To the Governors of H.M. Prisons.

Education.

As it appears that the regulations for the Educational Instruction of prisoners (Circular 348), are not fully carried out, I am directed to instruct you to see that they are strictly complied with in future, and that all prisoners eligible for instruction are duly instructed.

You are specially directed to see that prisoners are duly examined and classified; that prisoners in Class I. are taught reading collectively (two lessons weekly of half-an-hour each) and receive the same amount of cellular teaching in writing and arithmetic as that given to the other prisoners in three subjects; that the cellular instruction of prisoners in Class II. shall not be less than two lessons weekly of a quarter of an hour each; and that juveniles shall be instructed as provided for in Regulation No. VIII.

By order,
S. H. DOUGLAS,
Secretary.

General Prisons Board, Dublin Castle,
20th January, 1899.

To the Governors (or other officers in charge) of H.M. Local Prisons.

In continuation of Circular Memo. of 6th instant, as to secular instruction of prisoners, I am directed to inform you that the examination and classification of prisoners are to be made on reception; that the instruction of those eligible for instruction is thereupon to be commenced at once; and that the restriction heretofore imposed, in the Classification Tables, upon such instruction during probation is no longer to be enforced.

Pending the issue of revised Classification Tables, those at present in use are to be amended by striking out the references to school instruction, as indicated in copies attached. (809).

By order,

S. H. DOUGLAS,

Secretary.

A copy of this Circular is to be handed to each Chaplain.

Copy of REGULATIONS for STATE INEBRIATE REFORMATORIES made by the LORD LIEUTENANT, under the INEBRIATES ACT, 1898.

By the Lord Lieutenant-General and General Governor of Ireland.

CADOGAN.

WE, George Henry, Earl Cadogan, Lord Lieutenant-General and General Governor of Ireland, in pursuance of the powers vested in Us by the Inebriates Act, 1898, and of all other powers thereunto enabling Us, do hereby make the following regulations for the rule and management of State Inebriate Reformatories in Ireland, and for the classification, treatment, employment, and control of persons sent thereto in pursuance of the said Act, and for their absence under licence:

1. Every inmate shall be subject to the general rules for the government of local prisons, except so far as they are inconsistent with the following regulations:—

2. Inmates shall pass through three stages, viz.:—First, Second, and Third.

3. An inmate, on admission, will be placed in the First Stage, and will remain in it for a period of six months.

4. During this stage an inmate will be strictly confined within the walls, and will be employed, as far as possible, in the open air, under the immediate supervision of an officer. He will not be promoted from this stage unless by his industry and conduct he has proved himself worthy of promotion.

5. An inmate may write a letter and receive a reply on admission, and subsequently while in this stage, at intervals of a fortnight, and he may also receive a visit once a fortnight, unless by misconduct he should forfeit these privileges.

6. An inmate in the Second Stage, which will also extend for six months, will be employed, as far as possible, in the open air, but not necessarily under the immediate supervision of an officer.

7. After passing the first three months in this stage with exemplary conduct, an inmate shall become eligible for employment in positions of trust in and about the reformatory, and during the last three months in this stage he may be permitted to take a walk outside the walls under escort.

B

8. An inmate, while in the second and subsequent stages, may write a letter and receive a reply once a week and may receive a visit at the same intervals.

9. An inmate, if by his industry and conduct he has proved himself worthy of promotion, shall be promoted to the Third Stage, and shall remain in that stage till released.

10. While in this stage an inmate shall, if possible, be employed as far as the circumstances of the reformatory allow, in such form of labour as he has either a desire to learn or shows a capacity for executing, regard being had, in all cases where possible, to his chances of employment on release.

11. An inmate, after serving not less than three months in this stage may be allowed to leave the reformatory occasionally on parole, without an escort, during such time as shall be prescribed by the Governor, acting on the recommendation of the medical officer.

12. An inmate, after serving not less than ~~three-six months in this stage~~, may be eligible for the *Intermediate Class.* In order to attain the intermediate class an inmate must (1) prove to the satisfaction of the governor and medical officer, by his exemplary conduct in the third stage, that there exists a reasonable hope of his remaining a total abstainer and becoming a good citizen; (2) find a responsible person who will undertake in writing the charge of the inmate, and who will periodically report how he is conducting himself. The name of the inmate, with that of his proposed guardian, and such other particulars as may be necessary will be laid before the visiting committee, or not less than two members thereof, who will thereupon, if they are satisfied that his discharge can take place without danger to society, submit his name to the General Prisons Board, for licence of the Chief Secretary.

13. The name of an inmate to whom a licence shall have been granted, will remain on the books of the reformatory, as being out on probation until the expiration of his sentence.

14. The Visiting Committee may, in any case of special importance or urgency, allow an inmate an additional visit or letter, or prolong the period of a visit.

15. Provision shall be made for the payment to an inmate of earnings from labour performed. Such earnings shall be regulated by marks, and shall in no case exceed 1d. per day. An inmate by misconduct will be liable to forfeit his earnings.

16. Shops may be erected for the employment of inmates in trades. An inmate will be required to work each week day not less than six nor more than eight hours, except on Saturday, when labour shall cease at dinner-time.

17. The Governor, acting on the recommendation of the medical officer, shall give direction with regard to labour of an inmate, and he will be responsible that the employment is suitable to the physical condition of an inmate, and shall do all in his power to promote the industrial training of the inmates.

18. An inmate shall be supplied with food according to the scale laid down.

19. Meals will be served in the mess-room, due regard being had to order, cleanliness, and comfort.

20. Smoking will be allowed in the day-room, or exercise yards and grounds, during recreation hours, under regulations which shall be prescribed by the General Prisons Board. No smoking shall be allowed in the corridors, sleeping apartments, workshops, or kitchen.

21. An inmate shall be provided with a complete dress, sufficient for warmth, of such pattern as may be prescribed.

22. An inmate shall occupy a separate sleeping apartment at night, unless, for medical or special reason, it is necessary that he shall be placed in association. No inmate will be required to sleep on a plank bed.

23. Inmates may be associated at labour and exercise, and in the day-room for meals, and after the hours of labour.

24. Chess, draughts, dominoes, and other games that may be prescribed, may be used in the day-room.

25. Carefully selected newspapers and magazines shall be placed in the day-room for the use of the inmates.

26. Outdoor games may be organised in the open air on Saturday afternoons, and occasional entertainments, such as lectures and concerts, may be allowed from time to time.

27. . . . supply of books will be kept for inmates.

28. Ordinary diet:—

BREAKFAST:—

1 pint tea, 1 oz. butter, or bread. { 8 oz. oatmeal, 1 oz. Indian meal, 1 oz. rice, 1 pint milk, bread. } (made into stirabout).

DINNER:—

Sundays, ... { 8 oz. beef, boiled, 1 pint soup, potatoes or bread. { 4 oz. vegetables, 4 oz. oatmeal, 1 oz. rice.

Mondays and Saturdays { 1 pint pea soup, potatoes or bread.

Tuesdays and Thursdays { 8 oz. pork or 6 oz. mutton, potatoes, and vegetables. (made into stew.) or 3 oz. bacon, 8 oz. vegetables, potatoes or bread.

Wednesdays and Fridays { 1 pint milk, 1 oz. butter, potatoes or hallumean, or bread. or 8 oz. fish, 1 pint suffe, potatoes or bread.

SUPPER:—

{ 1 pint cocoa, 1 oz. butter, bread.

Bread and potatoes to be unlimited.
Tea—1 oz. tea, 8 oz. milk, and 1 oz. sugar for each person.
Cocoa—1 oz. cocoa, 8 oz. milk, and 1 oz. sugar for each person.
Pea soup—To be prepared as in local prisons.
Vegetables—Shall be onions, leeks, turnips, carrots, parsnips, cabbage, celery, or (preferably) a mixture of any of these.
Beef, mutton, pork, and bacon to weigh in the raw state, exclusive of bone, the weight specified in the Diet Table.
Fish dinner may be given in the form of fish pie.
The bread may be white or made of wholemeal.

TIME TABLE

Rise at 6.30 a.m.
Breakfast, 7.30 a.m.
Work, 8.30 a.m. till 12.30 p.m.
Dinner, 12.45 p.m. till 2 p.m.
Work, 2 p.m. till 6 p.m.
Supper, 6.0 p.m.
Sleeping apartment, 8.0 p.m.
Lights out—1st Stage, 9.30 p.m.
2nd and 3rd Stages, 10 p.m.

Given at Her Majesty's Castle of Dublin, this 16th day of March, 1899.

By His Excellency's Command,

D. HARREL.

APPENDIX

TO

TWENTY-FIRST REPORT OF THE GENERAL PRISONS BOARD.

PART II.

EXTRACTS FROM REPORTS BY SUPERIOR OFFICERS
OF CONVICT PRISONS.

MOUNTJOY CONVICT PRISON.

I.—MALE PRISON.

FROM GOVERNOR'S REPORT.

The subordinate officers have, with few exceptions, been well-conducted, attentive, and diligent. Three warders were found guilty of serious breaches of discipline and regulations, for which two were dismissed, and one permitted to resign. The chief and principal warders have performed their duties with zeal and intelligence.

There were 176 convicts in custody on the 1st April, 1898, 98 were received during the year under new sentences of penal servitude ; 5 military convicts (Irishmen) were received from English convict prisons ; 24 were received on forfeiture or revocation of licences ; 21 on transfer from Cork and Maryborough Prisons ; and 1 returned from Dundrum Criminal Lunatic Asylum. Fifty-four were released on licences ; 3 discharged on commutation of sentence ; 52 removed to Maryborough Prison ; 3 to Criminal Lunatic Asylum, and 1 died ; 211 remained in custody on the 31st March, 1899.

The convicts have been generally well-behaved, and amenable to rules and discipline, and they have been, on the whole, diligent and painstaking in the performance of their work.

They have been principally employed at indoor trades, as in preceding year, viz. :—tailoring, shoemaking, carpentry, coopering, baking, smithwork, tin-work, &c., and such as are incapable, from age or other cause of learning trades have been employed at mat-making, gardening, &c.

There have not been any escapes or attempts to escape during the year.

The buildings have been kept in good repair by prison labour.

The Chaplains have, as usual, attended regularly during the year, and have appeared to take deep interest in the spiritual and moral welfare of the convicts committed to their care. Three of the Chaplains are influential members of Prisoners' Aid Societies, and all have been ever ready to assist, on release, those desirous of earning their living honestly.

The probation convicts who cannot read, write and calculate, are taught by schoolmasters, in their cells, during each forenoon, on week-days, for the first nine months of their sentences, and the convicts who work in association during the day, and whose education is defective to the same extent, are taught for an hour each week evening, in classes, in a properly equipped school-room. The vast majority of the convicts appear to appreciate the educational advantages afforded to them, and endeavour to improve themselves. The schoolmasters have been diligent and attentive.

Library books are changed daily, during dinner hour, for the convicts, by one of the schoolmasters, and reading, during non-working hours, is encouraged.

I certify that the rules laid down for the government of the prison have been adhered to, except in such cases as have been brought to the notice of the General Prisons Board.

FROM PROTESTANT EPISCOPALIAN CHAPLAIN'S REPORT.

I have the honour of submitting my report for the past year, and have pleasure in stating that everything has gone on satisfactorily in my department, and that I can report most favourably of those committed to my charge. Thanking the Governor and staff of the gaol for ready co-operation in the discharge of sacred duties.

FROM ROMAN CATHOLIC CHAPLAINS' REPORT.

In submitting our report for the year ended March, 1899, it gives us much pleasure to bear testimony to the very satisfactory condition of the prisoners under our spiritual care. Their general conduct was good, and their attention to their religious duties was all that could be expected.

The discipline of the prison was well maintained during the past twelve months, and the breaches of it were, we are glad to say, comparatively few.

To the Governor, the medical officers, and the other officers with whom our duties brought us in contact, we beg to tender our sincere thanks for the kindness received from them on all occasions.

FROM PRESBYTERIAN CHAPLAIN'S REPORT.

I have to report that the prisoners under my care have been most attentive to the instructions imparted to them. I have also found them very amenable to any counsel I have thought it necessary to give them from time to time. Cases of insubordination or breaches of rules have been very rare among them, and I believe the men have honestly tried to reform themselves.

FROM MEDICAL OFFICER'S REPORT.

During the year there were 34 warders admitted into the Prison Hospital, chiefly for influenza and bronchitis. One warder—suffering from heart disease—was discharged the service on medical grounds. There was no death.

There were 131 convicts treated in hospital during the year. The principal ailments were:—Constipation, debility, influenza, catarrh, rheumatism, bronchitis, colic, diarrhœa, tonsillitis, dyspepsia, and wounds. Two convicts died, one was discharged from prison on medical grounds, and four were removed to the Criminal Lunatic Asylum. The daily average number of convicts treated in hospital was 11·147, as extern patients, 7·054.

During the year the health of the officers and the prisoners was generally good, and careful attention was paid to the sanitary arrangements of the prison.

II.—FEMALE PRISON.

FROM SUPERINTENDENT'S REPORT.

The subordinate officers have been well conducted and attentive to their duties during the year.

The convicts, who are principally employed at cleaning, cooking for convicts and local prisoners, gardening, needlework, and knitting, have been exceptionally well conducted.

Valuable assistance continues to be given to the Roman Catholic and Protestant Chaplains in the religious and moral instruction of the prisoners, by the Sisters of Charity and the Protestant lady visitor.

The secular instruction is conducted by the school mistress with most satisfactory results.

I certify that the rules laid down for the government of the prison have been complied with, except, in such cases as have been reported to the Board.

FROM PROTESTANT EPISCOPALIAN CHAPLAIN'S REPORT.

I have the honour of submitting my report of this prison for the past twelve months; and find nothing, during that period deserving special notice. I mention with approbation the conduct of those attending my ministrations; and always notice, during my visits to the gaol, the earnestness and assiduity of those responsible for the maintenance of discipline in the discharge of their duties.

FROM ROMAN CATHOLIC CHAPLAINS' REPORT.

In presenting our report for the year ended March, 1899, it affords us very sincere pleasure to be able to speak most favourably of the condition of the prisoners committed to our charge. Their conduct was very good; and their attention and devotion in chapel edifying.

The prison discipline, whilst being efficiently maintained, was administered in a spirit of kindness, and this we feel confident accounts for the cheerful and docile dispositions of the prisoners.

We desire to record, once more, our appreciation of the invaluable services rendered by the Sisters of Charity who so kindly visited and instructed the prisoners.

To the Lady Superintendent and the other officers of the Prison we return our best thanks for their kindness to us, and for the assistance rendered to us in the discharge of our duties.

FROM PRESBYTERIAN CHAPLAIN'S REPORT.

I am happy to be able to report that no Presbyterian Female Prisoner has been confined in this prison during the year.

FROM MEDICAL OFFICER'S REPORT.

There have been but few cases of serious illness among the members of the staff; but I regret to say that two convicts died during the past twelve months. The cause of death in each of these cases was tubercular enteritis, and every precaution was taken to prevent the spreading of the disease.

Influenza has as usual been prevalent, and was in one case followed by pneumonia, the other cases, however, were of a mild nature.

MARYBOROUGH CONVICT PRISON.

FROM THE GOVERNOR'S REPORT.

The conduct of the subordinate officers has, with one exception, been very satisfactory. One clerk joined the staff from Londonderry Prison; four second class warders joined from Mountjoy Prison; one from Tralee Prison; one clerk transferred on promotion to Armagh Prison; one clerk transferred to Londonderry Prison without change of rank; one second class warder transferred to Mountjoy Prison; and one second class warder dismissed the service for drunkenness.

There were in custody on 1st January, 1898:—Invalids, 27; in Intermediate Class, 11; and in Ordinary Labour Class, 67. Total—105. Received during year—Into Invalid Class, 2; into Intermediate Class, 32; and into Labour Class, 66.

Removed and discharged during the year—From Invalid Class, 21; from Intermediate Class, 33; and from Labour Class, 47. Remaining in custody on 31st December, 1898—Invalids, 8; Intermediate Class, 10; Ordinary Labour Class, 86. Total—104. During this period one invalid was removed to Dundrum Asylum. It will be observed that the numbers in Invalid Class have very considerably decreased, but this decrease is not entirely attributable to discharges or to restoration to health, as 10 were specially removed to Mountjoy prison to afford much-needed accommodation for additional convicts of the Labour Class.

It is gratifying to state that there are now only 8 invalid convicts in custody, as compared with 51, which number of invalids were in this prison when I took charge of it on 1st October, 1892.

On the morning of 21st October, 1898, two convicts attempted to escape by running away from their working party whilst employed building the boundary wall of farm. The convicts were promptly pursued by warders, re-captured, and conveyed back to the prison.

With this single exception, it is gratifying to be able to report that the conduct and industry of the convicts employed on farm and boundary walls have been highly satisfactory. The amount of permanent and enduring work performed by them has surprised persons who have have had an opportunity of observing them at their work.

The care displayed by them in their treatment of growing crops is very astonishing, when the antecedents of many of them are taken into consideration. Cases of misconduct are very few in number and slight in degree, which I attribute largely to the fact of their taking an active interest in their work, and being so much occupied in their various employments, they do not appear to think of mischief or misconduct.

Cases of violence or insubordination are unknown, and, whilst maintaining discipline, yet the warders in charge have no trouble ; they have merely to point out what they require to have done ; thus there is no conflict and no serious misconduct, such as was my unhappy experience when convicts were employed in less congenial occupations, when pressure had to be resorted to and gross misconduct prevailed.

The employment on the land is salutary, useful, and educational ; even the city-reared take a lively interest in their work. The habits of industry acquired must be highly beneficial to many in an agricultural country.

The crops grown were potatoes, barley, turnips, cabbages, onions, and the various table vegetables. We sold largely of cabbages, onions, cabbage plants and onion plants, as well as barley, potatoes, and turnips. Our potato crop last year was considered phenomenal ; in many cases nine potatoes weighed 14 lbs. It may be said that potatoes so large were not the most suitable for table, but they at least afforded sure indication of the produce, and, with care, we experienced no difficulty in cooking them thoroughly.

I sprayed the whole crop twice, and some three times, with a preparation of sulphate of copper and lime. Little or no blight appeared either on stalks or tubers. I have sprayed regularly for last four years, with most beneficial results. Some of the farmers are now adopting it, and at their meetings quote the prison as an example of what may be attained under what were, two years ago, very unpromising conditions of soil and surroundings. We disposed of 121 tons of potatoes during the year. The net profit from transactions in connection with the farm amounted to £192. The total sales for farm produce and from pigs reared on the produce of the farm amounted to £419 7s. 9d.

The conduct of the prisoners in the Intermediate class has been exceedingly satisfactory. I continue to communicate with the clergymen of the parish in which they may be about to reside after discharge, requesting their kind consideration and best influences on behalf of such prisoners. From some I receive satisfactory replies, and from none unfavourable. The information obtained enables me to conclude that those who adopt a country life and pursuits earn their livelihood by honest industry, whereas those who return to their former associations in cities are exposed to great danger of relapse.

The invalid prisoners, when not actually incapacitated, were employed cleaning prison, and as tailoring, making and repairing clothing. Their conduct has been uniformly good, although some of them are occasionally eccentric.

The prison buildings have been kept in a good state of repair, all necessary work being done by convicts under instruction of trade warders.

A party of twenty convicts of the labour class has been employed during the year excavating foundations for walls of new prison, and building in those foundations with concrete. At the present time this work has been taken over by a contractor, who has men employed preparing to proceed with the erection of the prison.

The chaplains have been zealous and attentive, willingly co-operating in every effort for the reformation of the prisoners whilst in prison, and for their welfare after discharge; they take a lively interest in seeing that suitable employment may be provided for the prisoners which may conduce to their advantage after they have left the prison.

The visiting physician, an eminent practitioner and a zealous officer, withdrew from the service of the prison in May of last year; the sole medical duties have since been discharged by the resident medical officer, who has been unremitting in his attention to the requirements of the prisoners.

The schools, morning and evening, continue to be conducted with satisfactory results, the progress made by the prisoners being very considerable, having regard to the opportunities and the time allowed for school.

The library is freely availed of, and the books annually provided are much appreciated. The schoolmaster acts as librarian.

I certify that the Rules laid down for the government of the Prison have been complied with to the best of my knowledge and belief.

The Visitors appointed by his Excellency the Lord Lieutenant visited the Prison on 13th April, 11th May, 8th June, 13th July, 10th August, 14th September, 12th October, 14th December, 1898, and on 11th January, 8th February, and 9th March, 1899.

I take the liberty to express my grateful acknowledgments of the valuable advice and assistance always willingly afforded by them in the interests of the Prison and for the benefit of the prisoners.

FROM PROTESTANT EPISCOPALIAN CHAPLAIN'S REPORT.

The behaviour of the prisoners attending the services of the Church of Ireland was during the past year uniformly quiet and respectful. A considerable number appeared attentive; those able to sing took an unusual interest in the musical portion of the services, and the singing was at times very good. Those who led requested to be allowed a short practice together on Saturday afternoons. The school continues to be useful to men whose education was neglected and who are anxious to learn. From the intern officers I received every assistance in their power.

FROM ROMAN CATHOLIC CHAPLAIN'S REPORT.

The conduct of the prisoners on the whole has been satisfactory. Their demeanour in the Chapel is really edifying, and a fair number of them are frequent communicants. They have taken great interest in the school business. The farming operations have been a great success. The prisoners prefer working a fair day's work on the farm rather than remain idle within the prison walls. This outdoor work destroys in a great measure the monotony of prison life, and makes them feel the term of their imprisonment pass far more quickly than under the old system. The Governor, Doctor, and the officials have been most courteous in their dealings with the Chaplains.

FROM MEDICAL OFFICER'S REPORT.

Since last report I have with regret to mention that Dr. D. B. Jacob resigned his appointment as Visiting Physician to this prison.

The health of officers and prisoners has been well maintained.

No death took place and no serious casualty occurred amongst the staff. One prisoner died who was in the invalid class, the cause being "Bright's disease." One case of insanity occurred—also an invalid class convict—and was transferred to Dundrum Lunatic Asylum.

The work provided here for convicts—farming—is, I think, the best suited to improve or maintain their bodily and mental health, as the occupation is congenial, interesting, and the result of the work so apparent to the prisoner's self. I can now remember cases of weak-minded prisoners whose minds might, I fear, have given way had they been employed at some indoor, irksome, or monotonous labour; and I may mention that malingering to shirk work is now here nearly unknown.

The new gravitation water supply, which will be in use in all probability in a few weeks, will, I am sure, give satisfaction and afford greater facilities for keeping the sanitary condition of the prison in the same thorough order as it existed during the year.

APPENDIX

TO

TWENTY-FIRST REPORT OF THE GENERAL PRISONS BOARD.

PART III.

PRISON TABLES.

Table I.—Return of Committals to the several Prisons
(For committals to

PRISONS.	On Remand and afterwards Discharged.	For trial at Assizes and Quarter Sessions, and to the re-call				A first commitment at Assizes and Quarter Sessions (not previously in Prison).	After Summary Conviction.
		Tried and Convicted.	Tried and Acquitted.	Remaining untried at end of year.	Otherwise disposed of.		
TOTAL, M. & F., { Local Prisoners, Convicts,	1,833	791	290	107	42	288	63,097

MALES.

Larger Prisons.

Armagh,							
Belfast,							
Castlebar,							
Clonmel,							
Cork, Male,							
Dundalk,							
Galway,							
Kilkenny,							
Kilmainham,							
Limerick, Male,							
Londonderry,							
Mountjoy,							
Sligo,							
Tralee,							
Tullamore,							
Waterford,							
Wexford,							

Minor Prisons.

Carrick-on-Shannon,							
Drogheda,							
Enniskillen,							
Mullingar,							
Omagh,							
Wicklow,							

Convict Prisons.

Maryborough,							
Mountjoy,							
Total Males,	1,556	640	298	94	42	278	61,010

FEMALES.

Larger Prisons

Armagh,							
Belfast,							
Castlebar,							
Cork, Female,							
Galway,							
Limerick, Female,							
Londonderry,							
Mountjoy, Female,							
Sligo,							
Tralee,							
Tullamore,							
Waterford,							
Wexford,							

Minor Prisons.

Carrick-on-Shannon,							
Drogheda,							
Enniskillen,							
Mullingar,							
Omagh,							
Wicklow,							

Convict Prisons.

Mountjoy, Female,							

General Prisons Board, Ireland.

, 1898, to 31st December, 1898.

(I.)

COMMITTED.					
Remaining on remand and of rem.	Other Classes	On Remand to Minor Prisons and other wards to Larger Prisons & usage charge	Total Committments (excluding Debtors and Prisoners under Civil Process).	Debtors and Prisoners under Civil Process	Grand TOTAL.
103	318	166	28,306	75	83,883
–	17	–	17	–	17

MALES.

FEMALES.

TABLE II.—RETURN of all PRISONERS received into LOCAL and CONVICT PRISONS, and of their Disposal, during the Year ended 31st December, 1898.

	Local Prisons			Convict Prisons			Total		
	Male	Fe-male	Total	Male	Fe-male	Total	Male	Fe-male	Total
Number at the {in Local Prisons									
commencement {On bail									
of the year {in Convict Prisons									
RECEIVED:—									
Under Committals, not having been in the custody of other Government:—									
Remanded and discharged									
Remanded or received at end of year									
For Trial at Assizes and Sessions, and in the result—									
Tried and convicted									
Tried and acquitted									
Remaining committed at end of the year									
Otherwise disposed of									
Convicted at Assizes and Sessions (not previously in Prison)									
Convicted summarily									
Want of sureties									
Debtors and Civil Process									
Naval and Military offenders									
Under sentence									
Military Convicts on transfer from English District Prisons									
From Lunatic Asylums (until Convict Prisons)									
Total									
Total Committals, &c.									
Received in Convict Prison after conviction (under Penal Servitude Act, 1864, or revocation of Licence)									
Total									
GROSS TOTAL									
DISPOSED OF:—									
Discharged on expiration of sentence or committal									
Discharged on bonded									
Discharged on pardon, remission of sentence, or mitigation of sentence									
Removed to Schools or Reformatories									
Removed to Lunatic Asylums									
Committed suicide									
Died									
Executed									
Total									
Remaining at the end of the year:—									
In custody									
Out on bail									
GROSS TOTAL									

TABLE III.—NUMBER of PRISONERS in each LOCAL and CONVICT PRISON on the First Day of each Month during the Year ended 31st December, 1898 (at Unlock).

1898.

PRISONS	1st Jan.	1st Feb.	1st March	1st April	1st May	1st June	1st July	1st Aug.	1st Sept.	1st Oct.	1st Nov.	1st Dec.

MALES.

LOCAL PRISONS.
Larger Prisons.

FEMALES.

LOCAL PRISONS.
Larger Prisons.

50·00	10·	70·00
441·13	111·97	4.36 14
95·00	8·64	90·00
15·73	—	15·73
900·43	—	900·43
6·90	—	6·90
—	81·	81
96·17	—	96·17
77·90	15·03	97·03
180·43	—	180·43
164·90	—	164·90
90·94	—	90·94
—	66·73	66·73
900·53	96·94	1.11 75
964·78	—	915 73
—	9.57·99	757 99
63·40	16·90	72·
90·43	9·40	90·90
75·90	1.5·71	93 94
90·90	90·93	97·03
11·90	9·90	90·90
9·90	·97	9·79
4·90	1·99	9·90
7·15	·96	8·63
5 61	1·77	1·90
4·99	1·95	9·19
9 84	·97	9·71

TABLE V.—RELIGIOUS PERSUASIONS of CONVICTED CRIMINALS committed to the undermentioned Local Prisons during the year ended 31st December, 1898, and of the Convicts in custody at end of year. (Court-Martial prisoners excluded.)

PRISONS.	Protestant Episcopalians of Ireland.		Presbyterians.		Roman Catholics.		Other Religious Persuasions.		Total.	
	M.	F.	M.	F.	M.	F.	M.	F.	M.	F.
Local Prisons.										
Armagh, ...	173	66	64	7	563	814	9	-	783	887
Belfast, ...	1,352	773	1,617	897	1,916	1,807	9	-	4,902	3,575
Castlebar, ...	39	8	-	-	319	128	-	-	368	138
Clonmel, . . . ' .	11	-	-	- .	873	-	1	-	885	-
Cork, Male, . . .	44	- '	19	-	1,683	-	6 '	-	1,800	-
Cork, Female, . . .	-	69	-	96	-	1,974	-	-	-	1,161
Dundalk, ...	89	-	8	-	423	-	1	-	520	-
Galway, ...	9	3	-	-	530	175	1	-	648	178
Kilkenny, ...	62	-	3	-	632	-	-	-	890	-
Maryborough, . . .	78	-	9	-	1,895	-	39	-	1,699	-
Limerick, Male, . .	34	-	7	-	1,093	-	-	-	1,138	-
Limerick, Female, .	-	7	-	-	-	647	-	-	-	654
Londonderry, . . . ;	199	114	62	35	780	637	-	-	1,063	887
Mountjoy, ...	904	-	83	-	4,862	-	16	-	1,846	-
Mountjoy, Female, .	-	468	-	16	-	14,682	-	9	-	4,69?
Sligo, ...	62	9	1	-	456	468	5	8	515	117
Tralee, ...	11	1	-	-	520	134	3	-	534	134
Tullamore, . .	11	8	8	-	337	178	-	-	441	182
Waterford, . . .	9	1	1	-	682	489	-	-	687	401
Wexford, ...	6	-	9	-	501	123	1	-	818	123
Total Local Prisons.	2,899	1,411	1,189	68	17,312	10,879	68	6	66,526	11,220
Convict Prisons.										
Maryborough, .	11	-	6	-	85	-	-	-	101	-
Mountjoy, Male, .	51	-	19	-	116	-	8	-	593	-
Mountjoy, Female,	-	1	-	-	-	19	-	-	-	19
Total Convicts in custody on 31st Dec.	65	1	17	-	941	18	8	-	397	19

TABLE VI.—SENTENCES ON CONVICTED CRIMINAL PRISONERS committed 1898, and number of such Prisoners

(Cumulative sentences are referred to as equal to their entire length. Concurrent sentences

Prisons.	Death	Death (commuted)	Life	Penal Servitude for									
				20 Years	15 Years	12 Years	10 Years	14 Years	12 Years	11 Years	7 Years	10 Years	5 Years

Prisoners Committed

Criminal Prisoners other than

Larger Prisons.

Armagh,	2	—	—	—	—	—	—	—	—	—	—	—	—	—
Belfast,	1	—	3	—	—	—	—	—	—	—	—	—	3	—
Castlebar,	—	—	—	—	—	—	—	—	—	—	—	—	—	—
Clonmel,	1	—	—	—	—	—	—	—	—	—	—	—	—	—
Cork, Male,	1	—	1	—	—	—	—	—	—	—	—	—	—	—
Cork, Female,	—	—	—	—	—	—	—	—	—	—	—	—	—	—
Dundalk,	—	—	—	—	—	—	—	—	—	—	—	—	—	—
Galway,	—	—	—	—	—	—	—	—	—	—	—	—	1	—
Kilkenny,	1	1	—	—	—	—	—	—	—	—	—	—	—	—
Kilmainham,	—	—	—	—	—	—	—	—	—	—	—	—	—	—
Limerick, Male,	—	—	—	—	—	—	—	—	—	—	—	—	3	—
Limerick, Female,	—	—	—	—	—	—	—	—	—	—	—	—	—	—
Londonderry,	—	—	1	—	—	—	—	—	—	—	—	—	1	—
Mountjoy, Male,	—	—	—	—	—	—	1	—	—	—	—	—	—	—
Mountjoy, Female,	—	—	—	—	—	—	—	—	—	—	—	—	—	—
Sligo,	—	—	—	—	—	—	—	—	—	—	—	—	—	—
Tralee,	—	—	—	—	—	—	—	—	—	—	—	—	1	—
Tullamore,	—	—	—	—	—	—	—	—	—	—	—	—	—	—
Waterford,	—	—	—	—	—	—	—	—	—	—	—	—	—	—
Wexford,	—	—	—	—	—	—	—	—	—	—	—	—	—	—

Minor Prisons.

Carrick-on-Shannon,	—	—	—	—	—	—	—	—	—	—	—	—	—	—
Drogheda,	—	—	—	—	—	—	—	—	—	—	—	—	—	—
Enniskillen,	—	—	—	—	—	—	—	—	—	—	—	—	—	—
Mullingar,	—	—	—	—	—	—	—	—	—	—	—	—	—	—
Omagh,	—	—	—	—	—	—	—	—	—	—	—	—	—	—
Wicklow,	—	—	—	—	—	—	—	—	—	—	—	—	—	—

Prisoners Convicted

| All Prisons, | — | — | — | — | — | — | — | — | — | — | — | — | — | — |
| Total | 6 | 2 | 1 | — | — | — | 1 | — | — | — | — | — | 7 | — |

Prisoners in Custody on

Local Prisons,	6	1	—	—	—	1	—	1	—	—	—	—	—	—
Convict Prisons.														
Maryborough,	—	3	4	—	2	1	2	—	—	5	1	—	2	1
Mountjoy, Male,	—	17	9	—	—	12	—	—	—	—	—	—	47	—
Mountjoy, Female,	—	—	—	—	—	—	—	—	—	—	—	—	—	—
Total,	3	71	14	—	6	13	1	—	9	2	—	9	51	1

In addition to these there were nineteen male and two female convicts in Mountjoy convicts as to the under-mentioned Prisons during the year ending 31st December, in custody on 31st December, 1898.

(are reckoned as equal to one of them, or in the lower when they are of an equal length.)

							Imprisonment for								
7 Years	6 Years	3 Years	2 Years	1 Year	Total Sentences of Penal Servitude	6 Years and above	1 Year and above 18 Months	18 Months and above 12 Months	12 Months and above 9 Months	9 Months and above 6 Months	6 Months and above 3 Months	3 Months and above 1 Month	1 Month and above	Prisons.

during Year.

those Convicted by Courts-Martial.

Larger Prisons.
Armagh.
Belfast.
Castlebar.
Clonmel.
Cork, Male.
Cork, Female.
Dundalk.
Galway.
Kilkenny.
Kilmainham.
Limerick, Male.
Limerick, Female.
Londonderry.
Mountjoy, Male.
Mountjoy, Female.
Sligo.
Tralee.
Tullamore.
Waterford.
Wexford.

Minor Prisons.
Carrick-on-Shannon.
Drogheda.
Enniskillen.
Mullingar.
Omagh.
Wicklow.

by Courts-Martial.

All Prisons.

Total.

31st December, 1898.

Local Prisons.

Convict Prisons.
Maryborough.
Mountjoy, Male.
Mountjoy, Female.

Total.

Male and Mountjoy Female Convict Prisons, respectively, undergoing various terms under revocation of licence.

TABLE VI.—SENTENCES on CONVICTED CRIMINAL PRISONERS committed to 1898, and number of such Prisoners in

(Cumulative sentences are returned as equal to their united length. Concurrent sentences

Prisoners Committed

Criminal Prisoners other than

Larger Prisons.

Armagh, Belfast, Castlebar, Clonmel, Cork, Male, Cork, Female, Dundalk, Galway, Kilkenny, Kilmainham, Limerick, Male, Limerick, Female, Londonderry, Mountjoy, Male, Mountjoy, Female, Sligo, Tralee, Tullamore, Waterford, Wexford.

Minor Prisons.

Carrick-on-Shannon, Drogheda, Enniskillen, Mullingar, Omagh, Wicklow.

Prisoners Committed

All Prisons

Total

Prisoners in Custody on

Local Prisons

Convict Prisons.

Maryborough, Mountjoy, Male, Mountjoy, Female.

Total

the under-mentioned Prisons during the year ending 31st December, custody on 31st December, 1898—*continued.*

(are returned as equal to one of them, or to the longer when they are of unequal length.)

	Improvement for							Total Sentences of Imprisonment	Total Sentences	Prisons.
2 Weeks and above 1 Week	1 Week	4 Days	6 Days	1 Day	6 Days	1 Day	1 Day			

during Year.

those Convicted by Courts-Martial.

Larger Prisons.

Armagh. Belfast. Castlebar. Clonmel. Cork, Male. Cork, Female. Dundalk. Galway. Kilkenny. Kilmainham. Limerick, Male. Limerick, Female. Londonderry. Mountjoy, Male. Mountjoy, Female. Sligo. Tralee. Tullamore. Waterford. Wexford.

Minor Prisons. Carrick-on-Shannon. Drogheda. Enniskillen. Mullingar. Omagh. Wicklow.

by Courts-Martial.

All Prisons.

Total.

31st December, 1898.

Local Prisons.

Convict Prisons. Maryborough. Mountjoy, Male. Mountjoy, Female.

Total.

TABLE VII.—NUMBER of CRIMINAL PRISONERS COMMITTED on conviction to
December, 1898, and the number of previous convictions incurred by
Prison under sentence.—Court-Martial Prisoners excluded.

PRISONS.	Number who had previously been in any Prison											
	Once.		Twice.		Thrice.		Four times.		Five times.		Six to Ten times.	
	M.	F.	M.	F.	M.	F.	M.	F.	M.	F.	M.	F.
Larger Local Prisons.	M.	F.	M.	F.	M.	F.	M.	F.	M.	F.	M.	F.
Armagh, . .	57	21	82	25	37	19	34	14	47	24	6	11
Belfast, . . .	438	163	377	117	163	91	161	73	163	65	551	176
Clonakilty, . .	61	16	8	4	16	9	9	5	7	6	21	16
Clonmel, . .	60	-	63	-	40	-	53	-	34	-	73	-
Cork, Male, .	223	-	144	-	103	-	63	-	79	-	261	-
Cork, Female, .	-	63	-	50	-	66	-	53	-	66	-	136
Dundalk, . .	70	-	67	-	43	-	62	-	17	-	72	-
Galway, . .	68	23	65	16	39	18	30	9	18	10	39	62
Kilkenny. .	21	-	11	-	18	-	8	-	9	-	9	-
Kilmainham, .	223	-	270	-	116	-	76	-	94	-	163	-
Limerick, Male,	163	-	74	-	138	-	63	-	61	-	146	-
Limerick, Female,	-	67	-	38	-	77	-	61	-	18	-	64
Londonderry, .	16	63	97	37	63	67	49	16	39	9	118	31
Mountjoy, Male,	471	-	325	-	265	-	121	-	168	-	811	-
Mountjoy, Female, .	-	670	-	393	-	313	-	311	-	390	-	631
Sligo, . . .	67	16	48	30	31	10	23	3	13	9	40	6
Tralee, . . .	83	23	63	9	63	6	39	6	16	6	38	10
Tullamore, . .	79	16	66	15	60	7	23	7	18	7	61	64
Waterford, . .	60	69	69	37	38	23	57	30	53	16	61	69
Wexford, . .	99	13	33	11	11	8	19	8	16	4	39	16
Minor Prisons.												
Carrick-on-Shannon, .	4	1	7	3	6	1	6	1	11	9	13	6
Drogheda, . .	30	13	31	6	71	1	13	8	10	9	14	6
Enniskillen, . .	13	3	13	6	9	3	8	8	6	4	14	7
Mullingar, . .	39	13	17	11	10	7	13	3	11	7	39	13
Omagh, . .	9	3	22	3	22	3	16	6	6	7	33	31
Wicklow, . .	19	1	13	6	6	3	8	1	3	-	6	3
Total committed to Local Prisons.	2659	1169	1913	613	1356	622	974	629	885	651	2518	1114
Convict Prisons. [*]												
Maryborough,	-	-	-	-	-	-	-	-	-	-	-	-
Mountjoy, Male,	-	-	-	-	-	-	-	-	-	-	-	-
Mountjoy, Female, .	-	-	-	-	-	-	-	-	-	-	-	-
Total received direct into Convict Prisons	-	-	-	-	-	-	-	-	-	-	-	-
GRAND TOTAL.	2659	1169	1913	613	1356	622	974	629	885	651	2518	1114

[*] Convicts committed under fresh sentences are accounted.

												Armagh.
												Belfast.
												Castlebar.
												Clonmel.
												Cork, Male.
												Cork, Female.
												Dundalk.
												Galway.
												Kilkenny.
												Kilmainham.
												Limerick, Male.
												Limerick, Female.
												Londonderry.
												Mountjoy, Male.
												Mountjoy, Female.
												Sligo.
												Tralee.
												Tullamore.
												Waterford.
												Wexford.
												Minor Prisons.
												Carrick-on-Shannon.
												Drogheda.
												Kinsale.
												Mullingar.
												Omagh.
												Wicklow.

TABLE VIII.—RETURN of PRISONERS within each of the following
on the 31st
(Court Martial

PRISONS.	Under 12 years.		12 years and under 16.		16 and under 21.		21 and under 30.		30 and under 40.	
	M.	F.	M.	F.	M.	F.	M.	F.	M.	F.
Larger Local Prisons.										
Armagh, ...	-	-	-	-	3	1	14	8	19	1
Belfast, ...	-	-	-	-	60	8	117	43	80	24
Castlebar, ...	-	-	-	-	2	-	11	-	6	-
Clonmel, ...	-	-	-	-	6	-	22	-	20	-
Cork, Male, . . .	-	-	-	-	20	-	60	-	35	-
Cork, Female. . .	-	-	-	-	-	1	-	20	-	23
Dundalk, ...	-	-	1	-	10	-	3	-	3	-
Galway, ...	-	-	-	-	5	-	60	5	17	6
Kilkenny, ...	-	-	-	-	6	-	19	-	19	-
Kilmainham, . . .	-	-	1	-	16	-	60	-	21	-
Limerick, Male, . .	-	-	-	-	24	-	30	-	30	-
Limerick, Female, .	-	-	-	-	-	1	-	13	-	6
Londonderry, . . .	-	-	-	-	15	-	37	7	30	10
Mountjoy, ...	1	-	3	-	34	-	140	-	77	-
Mountjoy, Female,	-	-	-	-	-	17	-	73	-	72
Sligo, ...	-	-	-	-	6	1	22	3	13	6
Tralee, ...	-	-	-	-	3	1	20	1	10	1
Tullamore, . . .	-	-	-	-	5	-	17	2	23	3
Waterford, . . .	-	-	-	-	4	1	13	11	27	6
Wexford, ...	-	-	-	-	4	-	14	-	17	3
Minor Prisons.										
Carrick on Shannon, .	-	-	-	-	-	-	-	-	3	-
Drogheda, . . .	-	-	1	-	1	1	6	-	1	-
Enniskillen, . . .	-	-	-	-	-	-	6	-	6	-
Mullingar, . . .	-	-	-	-	1	-	-	1	3	-
Omagh, ...	-	-	-	-	-	-	1	-	-	-
Wicklow, ...	-	-	-	-	-	-	-	-	1	-
Total Local Prisons, .	1	-	6	-	626	32	623	179	633	180
Convict Prisons.										
Maryborough, . . .	-	-	-	-	10	-	20	-	25	-
Mountjoy, Male, . .	-	-	-	-	5	-	54	-	42	-
Mountjoy, Female, .	-	-	-	-	-	1	-	5	-	7
Total Convict Prisons, .	-	-	-	-	15	1	80	5	60	7
GRAND TOTAL, . .	1	-	6	-	942	54	718	181	691	187

Periods of Age remaining in each of the Local and Convict Prisons
December, 1898.

(prisoners excluded.)

45 and under 50.		50 and under 60.		60 and above.		Age not ascertained.		Total		Prisons.
M.	F.	M.	F.	M.	F.	M.	F.	M.	F.	Larger Local Prisons.
7	6	3	6	3	3	-	-	77	16	Armagh.
41	29	46	30	3	4	-	-	125	134	Belfast.
-	6	-	-	1	1	-	-	12	5	Castlebar.
7	-	2	-	2	-	-	-	44	-	Clonmel.
13	-	11	-	6	-	-	-	176	-	Cork, Male.
-	20	-	6	-	1	-	-	-	58	Cork, Female.
10	-	1	-	3	-	-	-	45	-	Dundalk.
10	2	1	3	1	1	-	-	43	17	Galway.
10	-	5	-	6	-	-	-	59	-	Kilkenny.
10	-	13	-	7	-	-	-	100	-	Kilmainham.
12	-	5	-	5	-	-	-	90	-	Limerick, Male.
-	7	-	3	-	2	-	-	-	26	Limerick, Female.
14	5	9	3	6	7	-	-	105	25	Londonderry.
29	-	17	-	13	-	-	-	274	-	Mountjoy.
-	11	-	6	-	7	-	-	-	58	Mountjoy, Female.
5	1	4	1	-	5	-	-	43	14	Sligo.
4	3	9	-	5	-	-	-	44	6	Tralee.
3	3	5	-	6	-	-	-	64	14	Tullamore.
9	4	6	1	-	-	-	-	60	22	Waterford.
1	6	9	-	2	1	-	-	60	6	Wexford.
										Minor Prisons.
3	-	-	-	-	-	-	-	4	-	Carrick-on-Shannon.
-	-	1	-	-	-	-	-	7	1	Drogheda.
-	-	-	-	-	-	-	-	4	-	Enniskillen.
1	-	-	-	-	1	-	-	6	2	Mullingar.
-	-	-	-	-	-	-	-	1	-	Omagh.
-	-	-	-	6	-	-	-	3	-	Wicklow.
218	165	139	30	64	35	-	-	1764	399	Total Local Prisons.
										Convict Prisons.
19	-	9	-	4	-	-	-	146	-	Maryborough.
13	-	13	-	71	-	-	-	623	-	Mountjoy, Male.
-	4	-	2	-	-	-	-	-	39	Mountjoy, Female.
41	4	63	1	89	-	-	-	337	39	Total Convict Prisons.
377	185	160	32	98	90	-	-	2,103	514	GRAND TOTAL.

TABLE IX.—RETURN of Educational Attainments of Convicted Criminal
December, 1898, and Results

Prisons.	I. Condition of Convicted Criminal Prisoners committed during year, excluding those convicted by Courts-Martial.						II. Information regarding th			
	Unable to either Read or Write	Able to Read and Write Imperfectly	Able to Read and Write well	Superior Instruction	Education not ascertained	Total Number of Educational during the year	Average number of Prisoners under Instruction daily	Average Number of Hours of Instruction daily	Condition of at beginning of committal day: (a) Wholly Ignorant	(b) Able to Read	(c) Able to Read and Write

MALES.

Local Prisons.

Armagh,										
Belfast,										
Castlebar,										
Clonmel,										
Cork, Male, {Local Prisoners, {Convicts.										
Dundalk,										
Galway,										
Kilkenny,										
Kilmainham,										
Limerick, Male,										
Londonderry,										
Mountjoy,										
Sligo,										
Tralee,										
Tullamore,										
Waterford,										
Wexford,										
TOTAL LOCAL PRISONS										
Convict Prisons.										
Maryborough,										
Mountjoy,										
TOTAL CONVICT PRISONS										
Grand Total, Males,										

FEMALES.

Local Prisons.

Armagh,										
Belfast,										
Castlebar,										
Cork, Female,										
Galway,										
Limerick, Female,										
Londonderry,										
Mountjoy, Female,										
Sligo,										
Tralee,										
Tullamore,										
Waterford,										
Wexford,										
TOTAL LOCAL PRISONS										
Convict Prison.										
Mountjoy, Female,										
TOTAL CONVICT PRISON										
Grand Total, Females,										

Condition of Prisoners at end of Year, or on Discharge during Year.												
(a) Number of the "Wholly Ignorant,"				(b) Number of those "able to Read"			(c) Number of those "able to Read and Write"		(d) Number of those "able to Read, Write, & Calculate"			
Who learned to Read.	Who learned to Read and Write.	Who learned to Read, Write, and Calculate.	Remaining Wholly Ignorant.	Who learned to Write.	Who learned to Write and Calculate.	Remaining unable to Write or Calculate.	Who learned to Calculate.	Remaining unable to Calculate.	Who have improved in their knowledge.	Who have made no progress.		Total.
MALES.												
–	–	3	1	–	6	–	–	–	94	–		[illegible]
7	14	[illegible]	[illegible]	14	[illegible]	18	[illegible]	[illegible]	[illegible]	[illegible]		[illegible]
11	4	[illegible]	[illegible]	6	18	1	[illegible]	1	[illegible]	3		[illegible]
4	7	6	6	–	6	–	3	–	[illegible]	11		179
12	[illegible]	7	18	14	[illegible]	4	30	4	[illegible]	6		[illegible]
[illegible]	[illegible]	[illegible]	[illegible]	[illegible]	[illegible]	[illegible]	[illegible]	[illegible]	[illegible]	[illegible]		[illegible]
129	76	58	143	73	154	73	[illegible]	47	702	270		[illegible]
1	–	–	3	67	[illegible]	7	[illegible]	[illegible]	[illegible]	11		[illegible]
1	–	4	4	–	6	4	11	1	[illegible]	5		[illegible]
8	–	5	7	37	10	11	36	[illegible]	[illegible]	16		[illegible]
129	76	58	150	140	164	84	[illegible]	116	[illegible]	[illegible]		2,847
FEMALES.												
[illegible]	[illegible]	[illegible]	[illegible]	[illegible]	[illegible]	[illegible]	[illegible]	[illegible]	[illegible]	[illegible]		[illegible]

Table X.—Diseases for which Prisoners on Sick Report have been treated in the undermentioned Prisons during the Year ended 31st December, 1898.

Description of Disease	Total Number of Cases	Queen's Prison — Kingstown Female	Mountjoy	Maryborough	Wexford	Waterford	Tullamore	Tralee	Sligo	Mountjoy Female	Mullingar	Londonderry	Limerick Female	Limerick Male	Kilmainham	Kilkenny	Galway	Dundalk	Cork Female	Cork Male	Clonmel	Castlebar	Belfast	Armagh
I. Zymotic:—																								
Typhus																								
Enteric Fever																								
Influenza																								
Variola																								
Erysipelas																								
Other Zymotic Diseases																								
II. Parasitic:—																								
Scabies																								
Ascarides																								
Ringworm																								
Other Parasitic Affections																								

III. Bladder—
Cancer,
Alcoholism,
Delirium Tremens,
Insomnia,
Mania from Drink.

IV. Constitutional:—
Rheumatic Fever,
Rheumatism,
Cancer,
Phthisis,
Scrofula,
Syphilis,
Anæmia,
Diabetes,
Other Constitutional Disease

V. Developmental:—
Senile Decay,

TABLE X.—DISEASES for which PRISONERS on SICK REGISTERS have been treated in, the undermentioned Prisons—*continued.*

Number of Cases in each Prison.

Description of Disease	LOCAL PRISONS.																			CONVICT PRISONS.			Total Number of Cases.
	Armagh.	Belfast.	Cavan.	Clonmel.	Cork, Male.	Cork, Female.	Dundalk.	Galway.	Kilkenny.	Kilmainham.	Limerick, Male.	Limerick, Female.	Londonderry.	Mountjoy.	Mountjoy, Female.	Sligo.	Tralee.	Tullamore.	Waterford.	Maryborough.	Mountjoy.	Mountjoy, Female.	
VI. Local:—																							
A.—Diseases of Nervous System.																							
Apoplexy,																							
Paralysis,																							
Seizure,																							
Epilepsy,																							
Neuralgia,																							
Paraplegia,																							
Hysteria,																							
Insanity,																							
Other Diseases of Brain and Nervous System,																							
B.—Diseases of Organs of Special Sense.																							
Opthalmia,																							
Keratitis,																							

Conjunctivitis.
Otitis.
Other Diseases of Eye or Ear.
—Diseases of Circulatory System.
Valvular Disease of Heart.
Aneurism.
Varicose Veins.
Syncope.
Other Diseases of Circulatory System.
D.—Diseases of Respiratory System.
Laryngitis.
Bronchitis.
Bronchitis Chronic.
Pneumonia.
Pleurisy.
Consumption of Lungs.
Asthma.
Haemoptysis.
Empyema.
Bronchial Catarrh.
Catarrh.
Other Diseases of Respiratory System.

TABLE X.—DISEASES for which PRISONERS on SICK REGISTER have been treated in the undermentioned Prisons—*continued.*

Number of Cases in each Prison.

Description of Diseases.	Armagh	Belfast	Castlebar	Clonmel	Cork, Male	Cork, Female	Dundalk	Galway	Kilkenny	Kilmainham	Limerick, Male	Limerick, Female	Londonderry	Monaghan	Monaghan, Female	Nenagh	Tralee	Tullamore	Waterford	Wexford	Maryborough	Mountjoy, Male	Mountjoy, Female	Total Number of Cases
1.—Diseases of Digestive System																								
Bronchitis																								
Quinsell																								
Tonsillitis																								
Dyspepsia																								
Hæmatemesis																								
Gastritis																								
Gastric Ulcer																								
Bilious Derangement																								
Liver Disease																								
Jaundice																								
Colic																								
Enteritis																								
Peritonitis																								
Diarrhœa																								
Constipation																								
Hernia																								

Piles.

Fistula in Ano.

Other Diseases of Digestive System.

F.—Diseases of Lymphatic System.

Lymphadenitis.

G.—Diseases of Urinary System.

Nephritis.

Prostatic Disease.

Catarrh of Bladder.

Cystitis.

Nephritis.

Bright's Disease.

Other Diseases of Urinary System.

H.—Diseases of Organs of Generation.

Urethritis.

Gonorrhœa.

Chancre.

Orchitis.

Disorders of Menstruation.

Other Diseases of Generative Organs.

TABLE X.—DISEASES for which PRISONERS on SICK REGISTER have been treated in the undermentioned Prisons—continued.

Description of Disease	LOCAL PRISONS. Number of Cases in each Prison.																						CONVICT PRISONS.				Total Number of Cases
	Armagh.	Belfast.	Carlickfergus.	Clonmel.	Cork, Male.	Cork, Female.	Derry.	Galway.	Kilkenny.	Kilmainham.	Limerick, Male.	Limerick, F. Female.	Londonderry.	Mullinger.	Mountjoy, Female.	Sligo.	Tralee.	Tullamore.	Waterford.	Wexford.	Maryborough.	Mountjoy.	Mountjoy, Female.	Total Number of Cases
I.—Diseases of Parturition.																								
Abortion.																								
Puerperal Convulsions.																								
Other Diseases of Parturition.																								
J.—Diseases of Bone and Organs of Locomotion.																								
Caries.																								
Arthritis.																								
Synovitis.																								
Rheum.																								
Bursitis.																								
Whitlow.																								
Lumbago.																								
Other Diseases of Organs of Locomotion.																								
L.—Diseases of Integumentary System.																								
Carbuncle.																								
Ulcer.																								
Phlegmon.																								
Pustule.																								
Lupus.																								

VII. Violence:—

Wounds,
Burns,
Contusions,
Sprains,
Dislocation,
Fracture,
Scalds,
Bite,
Otherwise,

VIII. Ill-defined and not specified:—

Anaemia,
Debility,
Dropsy,
Other Ill-defined Causes,

Total,

Number of Prisoners in Prison Hospital during year ended 31st Dec. 1889.

Daily average number in Hospital during year.

TABLE XI.—PARTICULARS of PRISONERS RELEASED on MEDICAL GROUNDS from LOCAL and CONVICT PRISONS during the Year ended 31st December, 1898.

[See Paragraph 135 of Report of Royal Commission, 1884.]

Name of Prison.	No.	Sex.	Initials of Prisoner.	Date of Committal.	Date of Reception.	Sentence.	Date of Release.	Disease or Cause on account of which released.	Whether above ordinary health or below perception.
Larger Local Prisons. Armagh,	1	F.	E.G.	12.10.98,	12.10.98,	1 c. with h.l.	22.10.98,	Old age and debility,	Before
	2	M.	A.V.	—	10.7.98,	Unlimited,	14.10.98,	Debility and loss of weight,	After
	3	M.	E.V.	—	18.7.98,	Do.,	11.10.98,	Do.,	Do.
Belfast,	4	F.	M.M'A.	12.12.97,	4.1.98,	14 days Imprisonment,	8.1.98,	Advanced prognosis,	—
	5	F.	M.C.	9.6.98,	14.4.98,	9 c. with h.l. and 2	4.11.98,	Debility and marine disease,	Before
	6	F.	C.D.	12.8.98,	12.8.98,	3 c. with h.l.	22.11.98,	Advanced prognosis,	—
Omagh,	7	F.	B.T.	28.2.98,	16.4.98,	2 c. with imp.	4.4.98,	A typh, infirm old woman,	Before
	8	M.	P.B.	2.3.98,	2.3.98,	1 c. with h.l.	14.4.98,	Partly typhus,	Unreadable
	9	F.	C.W.	—	6.4.98,	Indelible,	24.4.98,	Melancholia,	Before
	10	M.	P.Q.	1.12.97,	22.6.98,	2 c. with h.l.	12.10.98,	Senile decay.	Do.

General,	.	.								—
Cork Male,	31	M.	F. H.	.	22. 9. 85,	22. 9. 85,	2 o. mths. impt.	Syncope of cancer in face.	After	
Cork Female,	19	F.	L. L.	.	—	4. 11. 87,	Writ of attachment.	Gravid debility, &c.,	Do	
	18	F.	E. D.	.	4. 10. 86,	4. 10. 86,	1 c. mth. impt.	Advanced pregnancy,	.	
	14	F.	E. D.	.	2. 11. 86,	2. 11. 86,	1 c. mth. impt. or 2l. fine.	Do,	.	
Dundalk,	.	.						.	.	—
Galway,	15	F.	M. D.	.	3. 5. 86,	22. 6. 86,	1 c. mth. h. l.	Advanced pregnancy,	.	Before
	16	M.	W. J.	.	1. 6. 86,	18. 9. 86,	8 c. mth. impt. or £5 fine.	Heart disease,	.	
Kilkenny,	.	.	?					.		—
Kilmainham,	.	.								—
Limerick Male,	17	M.	M. C.	.	22. 6. 86,	4. 7. 86,	7 days and 2 c. mths. R. L.	Mitral disease and dropsy,	.	Before
Limerick Female,	18	F.	N. K.	.	23. 4. 86,	23. 3. 86,	1 mth. impt.	Advanced pregnancy,	.	
	19	F.	M. B.	.	27. 7. 88,	18. 6. 88,	7 days impt.	Do,	.	
	20	F.	E. H.	.	4. 6. 86,	23. 6. 86,	7 days impt.	Do,	.	
	21	F.	M. O'D.	.	23. 6. 86,	7. 10. 86,	1 mth. impt.	Do,	.	

TABLE XL, *continued.*—PARTICULARS of PRISONERS RELEASED on MEDICAL GROUNDS from LOCAL and CONVICT PRISONS during the Year ended 31st December, 1898.

[See Paragraph 136 of Report of Royal Commission, 1884.]

Name of Patient	Sex	Initials of Prisoner	Date of Conviction	Date of Reception	Sentence	Date of Release	Disease or Cause on account of which released	Whether since dead or alive, and whether restored to chief complaint
Lunkratony,	M.	F. McB.	6. 4. 97,	21. 3. 98.	42 days' imp. in default of payment of a debt amounting to £19 2s.	14. 5. 98.	Old age, general debility, and chronic bronchitis.	Before.
Memphory Local,	M.	D. R.	20. 12. 97,	20. 12. 97.	14 days or 20s.	8. 1. 98.	Rheumatism.	After.
	M.	J. L.	24. 2. 98.	24. 2. 98.	1 c. mth. h. l.	2. 3. 98.	Heart disease.	Before.
	M.	J. McL.	22. 6. 98.	22. 6. 98.	6 c. mths. h. l.	30. 7. 98.	Advanced disease of testicle.	Do.
Memphory Female,	F.	J. P.	10. 4. 98.	11. 4. 98.	3 c. mths. imp.	16. 4. 98.	Advanced pregnancy.	—
	F.	E. M.	6. 6. 98.	6. 6. 98.	9 c. mths. h. l.	7. 7. 98.	Do.	—
	F.	M. McG.	21. 6. 98.	21. 6. 98.	3 c. mths. h. l. 1 c. mth. h.l.	10. 8. 98.	Do.	—
	F.	J. F.	26. 8. 98.	26. 8. 98.	1 c. mth. imp.	14. 10. 98.	Pyræmia.	Before.
	F.	E. W.	—	21. 8. 98.	For trial.	11. 11. 98.	Chronic bronchitis.	Do.
	F.	F. W.	—	8. 7. 98.	Remand.	11. 7. 98.	Secondary syphilis.	Do.

Prison	No.	Sex	Initials			Sentence		Medical notes	Before/After
Sligo	82	F.	A. M.	7. 7. 86,	7. 7. 88,	21 days h. l.	16. 7. 84,	Typhus lever.	Before.
	33	M	P. P.	4. 1. 86,	3. 1. 87,	6 c. mths. h. l.	21. 1. 88,	Chronic ulcers, legs.	Do.
	34	F.	J. B.	26. 5. 86,	25. 8. 84,	1 c. mth. imp.	6. 16. 88,	Advanced pregnancy.	—
Tralee	33	M	M. G.	7. 2. 87,	2. 2. 86,	1 a. mth. h. l. or 20 ls. 6d.	18. 6. 86,	Hectic lever.	Before.
Tullamore	36	F.	R. H.	9. 8. 89,	9. 8. 86,	1 c. mth. imp.	19. 6. 86,	Advanced pregnancy.	—
	37	P.	M. McR.	17. 8. 88,	17. 8. 81,	14 days miable labour	18. 6. 86,	Do.	—
	38	M.	T. M.	18. 11. 87,	22. 11. 87,	To be detained until ordered to be discharged by Court.	7. 16. 86,	General debility.	After.
Waterford	39	M.	J. F.	4. 4. 86,	8. 4. 86,	9 mths. h. l.	6. 6. 86,	Playnlate sloughing ulcer of leg.	Before.
Wexford	40	M.	W. McC.	4. 2. 86,	10. 1. 86,	5 c. mths. h. l.	24. 3. 86,	Diarrhea.	Before.
	41	P.	K. C.	14. 1. 86,	14. 1. 86,	6 mths. imp.	7. 3. 86,	Advanced pregnancy.	—
	42	M	P. B.	13. 10. 86,	24. 8. 83,	6 mths. h. l.	12. 11. 84,	Broken down in health and unsuitable for prison lsts.	Before.
Minor Prisons, Carrickon-Shannon	—	—	—	—	—	—	—	—	—

TABLE XI., *continued.*—PARTICULARS of PRISONERS RELIEVED on MENTAL GROUNDS from LOCAL and CONVICT PRISONS during the Year ended 31st December, 1895.

[See Paragraph 136 of Report of Royal Commission, 1894.]

No.	Name of Prison	Sex	Initials of Prisoner	Date of Conviction	Date of Reception	Sentence	Date of Release	Disease or Cause on account of which relieved	Whether relieved under or after expiration of sentence
43	Drogheda	M.	N. B.	4. 3. 95.	4. 3. 95.	7 days imp.	7. 3. 95.	General debility.	Before.
44	Enniskillen	F.	M. D.	4. 7. 95.	4. 7. 95.	1. 7 days h. l. or fi.; 11. 3 days h. l. or fi.	7. 7. 95.	Advanced pregnancy.	—
45	Mullingar	M.	P. R.	19. 10. 95.	27. 10. 95.	7 days imp. or 12s.	29. 10. 95.	Bronchitis asthma.	Before.
	Omagh								—
	Wicklow								—
	Convict Prisons.								
	Maryborough								—
46	Mountjoy	M.	W. McD.	2. 12. 97.	18. 4. 97.	5 years p. s.	27. 10. 95.	Progressive implication of spinal cord ...	After.
47	Mountjoy Female	F.	C. D.	16. 7. 94.	21. 8. 94.	Death, commuted to p. s. for life	31. 12. 95.	Debility following dento pregnancy ...	After.

TABLE XII.—DEATHS in LOCAL and CONVICT PRISON and their CAUSES during the year ended 31st December, 1898.

(a) DEATHS EXCLUSIVE OF EXECUTION

Prison in which Death occurred.	No.	Sex	Initials of Name	Age	Date of Reception.	Date of Conviction.	Sentence.	Date of Death.	Cause of Death.	Whether Disease originated before or after reception into Prison.	General Health of Deceased on Reception into Local Prison.	Number of former Convictions.	Previous Occupation.
Local Prisons.													
Armagh.	1	M.	P. F.	61	4. 4. 98.	4. 3. 98.	3. 98. 24 mths. h.l. and 3 s. mths. or bail.	16. 3. 98.	Asthma.	Before.	Good.	Nil.	Labourer.
Do.	2	M.	J. W.	37	7. 4. 98.	1. 4. mth. h.l.	16. 4. 98.	Dropsy, depending on disease of liver.	Before.	Not good.	4	Labourer.
Belfast.									—	—	—	—	—
Castlebar.									—	—	—	—	—
Clonmel.									—	—	—	—	—
Cork Male.									—	—	—	—	—
Cork Female.	3	F.	M. R.	52	28. 11. 98.	28. 11. 98.	16 mth. imp.	3. 12. 98.	Pneumonia.	Before.	Fairly good.	4	Prostitute.
Dundalk.									—	—	—	—	—
Galway.									—	—	—	—	—
Kilmainham.	4	M.	W. W.	63	4. 10. 97.	19. 10. 97.	17a mths. h.l.	4. 5. 98.	Heart disease.	Before.	Fair.	10	Labourer.
Limerick Male.									—	—	—	—	—

TABLE XII.—*continued*—DEATHS In LOCAL and CONVICT PRISONS and their CAUSES during the year ended 31st December, 1898.

Prisons in which Death occurred	No.	Sex	Age	Initials of Name	Date of Reception	Date of Committal	Sentence	Date of Death	Class of Death	Whether Disease originated before or after Reception into Prison	General Health on first going into Local Prison	Number of Former Convictions	Previous Occupation
Limerick Fem.	4											NIL.	
London Derry.	5	m.	54	A.K.B	1. 95	11. 95	Carried.	17. 2. 94.	Suicide by strangulation.	Before.	Good.	6	Farmer.
Do.	6	m.	39	H. D.	6. 98.	7. 6. 98.	7 days A.L.	78. 6. 98.	Exhaustion after drink.		Not good.	3	Laborer.
Mountjoy.	7	f.		L. L.	12. 98.	12. 11. 98.	4c. mths A.L.	14. 12. 98.	Committed suicide.	Before.	Fair.	NIL.	Painter.
Do.	8	m.	70	W. M.	1. 10. 98.	1. 10. 98.	14 mth. A.L.	4. 11. 98.	Pneumonia.		Poison.		Mason.
Mountjoy Fem.													
Sligo													
Tralee	9	m.	43	H. M.	1 12. 98.	8. 12. 98.	1 c mth. A.I	10. 12. 98.	Failure of heart's action.	Before.	Good.	2	Engine driver.
Tullamore													
Waterford.	10	m.		J. M'C	11 93. 98.	14. 93. 98.	7 days imprt or 31s. fine.	14. 12. 98.	Cardiac failure after excessive drinking.	Before.	Good.	6	Laborer.
Wexford.													
River Prisons													
Carrick-on-Shannon											apparently good.		
Dundalk													
Enniskillen.													

Mullingar.												
Omagh.												
Wicklow.												
Convict Prison.												
Maryborough	11	m.	P.-M'L.	07yr.	b. 96.	b. 87.	5 years p.c.	b. 92.	Bright's disease of kidney.	After.	Ed known.	0	Dealer.
Mountjoy.	12	m.	J. H.	36 08.	12. 94.	12. 84.	Death, commuted to life p.s. and afterwards commuted to 14 years p.s.	14. 94.	Cardiac failure supervening on spinal paralysis.	After.	Good.	NIL.	Farmer.
Do.	13	m.	P. L.	71 08.	18. 93.	99. 10. 93.	5 years p.c. 14.	3. 90.	Pneumonia.	After.	Good.	0	Bookseller.
Mountjoy Fem.	14	f.	M. D.	30.	4. 98.	4. 92.	10 years p.c.	07. 4. 90.	Pulmonary disease of lumbrion.	Unknown.	Fair.	NIL.	Publican and Grocer.
Do.	15	f.	A. H.	44 72.	4. 98.	4. 98.	4 years p.c.	4. 12. 90.	Acute peritonitis.	After.	Indifferent.	0	No idea.

(b) Executions.

Clonmel.	1	m.	W.F.N.	28	16. 1. 94.	4. 2. 94.	To be executed by hanging	6. 4. 94.	Fracture of the cervical vertebrae and severing of the spinal cord.	—	Good.	1	Soldier.
Tullamore.	2	m.	P. H.	21	77. 10. 97.	14. 12. 97.	Death.	11. 1. 98.	Hanging.	—	Good.	NIL.	Farming.

* This man's imprisonment expired on 31.10.91, but as he was kept then unfit for discharge he remained in the prison hospital, where he died on 6.11.91.

TABLE XIII.—PARTICULARS of each case of INSANITY (amongst Prisoners)

(See paragraph 146 of Report)

Initials of Name.	Reg. No.	Sex.	Age (years).	Education.	Occupation previous to Conviction.	Crime or Charge.	Date of Conviction (if Convicted).	Sentence (if sentenced).	Place of Keeping had above a Local Prison.	
					ARMAGH.				**LOCAL**	
	-	-	-	-	-	-	-	-	-	
					BELFAST.					
J. M.	51	M.	30	R. W	Labourer,	Larceny,	—	For trial,	12. 1. 99	1
J. N.	150	M.	60	R.	Tramp,	Vagrancy,	12. 2. 99	1 c. mth. h.l.	12. 2. 99	2
M. P.	788	F.	30	do.	Servant,	do.	6. 3. 99	11 days h.l.	6. 3. 99	3
H. K.	2371	M.	30	do.	Labourer,	Assault,	6. 11. 97	6 c. mths. h.l.	6. 11. 97	4
J. M. L.	1460	M.	33	R. W.	do.	Using threats,	16. 6. 99	1 c. mth. bail,	16. 6. 99	5
J. K.	3741	M.	17	do.	Merchant,	Larceny,	72. 7. 99	14 days h.l.	6. 7. 99	6
S. M.	1916	M.	77	do.	Labourer,	do.	17. 6. 99	24 mths h.l.	17. 6. 99	7
					CASTLEBAR.					
S. H.	609	F.	50	R. W.	Dealer,	Larceny,	18. 7. 99	19 mths. h.l.	18. 7. 99	8
					CLONMEL.					
D. F.	119	M.	53	R. W.	Labourer,	I. Unlawfully having a revolver and 10 percussion caps in his possession.	26. 7. 99	I. 1 c. mth. h.l.	6. 8. 99	9
						II. Assault Police,	—	II. 14 days, h.l. to follow		
					CORK (Male).					
M. C.	1691	M.	45	R. W.	Cooper,	Assault and attempt to do bodily harm.	—	—	19. 1. 99	10
P. N.	4580	M.	63	ID.	Fisherman,	Drunk and incapable,	17. 6. 99	14 days h.l., or 10s. 6d fine.	17. 6. 99	11
J. S.	1197	M.	24	R. W.	Labourer,	I. Drunk and disorderly, II. Assault.	11. 7. 99	I. c. mth. h.l. II. c. mths. h.l.	11. 7. 99	12
J. F.	1478	M.	32	do.	do.	I. Drunk and disorderly, II. Assault Police. III. Assault.	13. 6. 99	I. 1 c days h.l. II. 1 c. mth. h.l. III. 1 do.	6. 6. 99	13
J. H.	1475	M.	44	do.	Tailor,	I. Larceny. II. do. III. do.	13. 9. 99	I. 7 c. mths. h.l. II. 7 do. III. 9 do.	6. 6. 99	14
P. L.	1799	M.	31	ID.	Ballad singer,	Arson,	—	Found insane and incapable of pleading. Ordered to be detained during pleasure of Lord Lieutenant.	16. 10. 99	15
					CORK (Female).					
A. D.	162	F.	11	Nil.	Homekeeper,	Larceny,	13. 6. 99	I. 10 c. mths. h.l. II. 10 do. III. 10 do. IV. 10 do. V. 10 do.	2. 1. 99	16
M. M C.	911	F.	36	R. W.	Prostitute,	I. Drunkenness, II. Breaking window	22. 3. 99	I. 7 days, or 11s. 6d. II. 1 c. mth cnp.	22. 6. 99	17
M. W.	603	F.	31	do.	do.	Charged with attempting to commit suicide,	—	For trial,	22. 7. 99	18
					DUNDALK.					
P. D.	700	M.	44	R. W.	Labourer,	Drunkenness,	1. 8. 99	7 days imp., or 4s,	22. 11. 99	19

in LOCAL and CONVICT PRISONS, during Year ended 31st December, of Royal Commission, 1884).

Verbal ... on Reception into a Local Prison.	Whether previously in use.	Length of Imprisonment previous to first symptoms of Insanity (the cases originating in Prison).	Form of Insanity.	Supposed cause of Insanity.	[Recovered Prison.]
PRISONS.			**ARMAGH.**		
—	—	—	—	—	—
			BELFAST.		
known.	Not known.	—	Dementia.	Not known.	•
do.	do.	—	Senile dementia.	do.	•
do.	do.	—	Mania.	Alcoholism.	•
do.	do.	5 months.	Delusional mania.	Syphilis.	•
known.	Yes.	—	Delusional insanity.	Not known.	•
do.	Not known.	—	Delusional mania.	do.	•
do.	do.	—	Religious mania.	do.	•
			CASTLEBAR.		
known.	Yes.	—	Recurrent mania.	Unknown.	—
			CLONMEL.		
Probably be- cause, brain tissue had not developed.	Not known.	14 days.	Acute mania.	Probably hereditary.	—
			CORK (Male).		
known.	Not known.	—	Alcoholic mania.	Drink.	—
do.	do.	—	Acute mania.	Not known.	—
Good.	No.	62 days.	do.	do.	—
known.	Not known.	—	do.	Vicious habits.	—
Good.	No.	65 days.	Sub-acute mania.	Not known.	—
Weak minded.	do.	—	Sub-Mania.	Hereditary.	—

TABLE XIII.—PARTICULARS of each case of INSANITY (amongst Prisoners) in LOCAL

Initials of Xtian.	Reg. No.	Sex	Age (Years)	Education.	Occupation previous to Conviction.	Crime or Charge.	Date of Conviction (if Convicted).	Sentence (if convicted).	Date of Recovery from Insanity in a Local Prison.	Re.
						GALWAY.				
M. O.,	181	F.	40	R.W.	Servant,	Maliciously break and injure a stove and two [indices], value £4l 6s.	16. 5. 68	3 c. mths. h.l.	24. 5. 68	10
K. M.,	670	F.	52	do.	Steal (improperly a servant). Robs to from according to his duties, &c.	12. 4. 68	3 c. mths. bail.	11. 4. 69	11
D M.,	351	F.	42	X.	Charwoman.	I. Drunk, . . . II. do., . III. Drunk and disorderly behaviour. IV. do., .	72. 4. 68 / 4. 4. 69 / 4. 6. 69 / 4. 6. 70	? days, or 1s. and 1s. 6d. / ? days, or 3s. and 1s. 6d. / 11 days, or 10s. 6d. and 1s. 6d. / 14 days, or 10s. 6d. and 1s. 6d.	11. 4. 68	71
B. K.,	421	M.	19	R.W. (Cong.)	Farmer's son.	Assault and beat Martin Flaherty.	7. 9. 68	1 c. mth. h.l.	4. 9. 68	13
J. R. D.,	771	M.	29	R.W.	Soldier,	Desertion from H. M.'s Twelfth Lancashire Regiment.	—	—	11. 11. 68	14
						KILKENNY.				
W. O.,	189	M.	38	R.W.	Labourer,	House-breaking, . .	18. 2. 68	4 c. mths. h.l., . .	28. 2. 68 after transfer.	15
J. F.,	322	M.	20	IR.	do.,	Assault and wounding, .	61. 3. 68	To be detained during H. M's pleasure.	16. 4. 68	16
W. D.,	790	M.	72	R.W.	do.,	I. Drunk on public street. II. do.,	2. 8. 69 / 11. 8. 70	14 days imp., or 12s., / 14 days imp., or 13s. 6d.	7. 18. 68	17
M. B.,	718	M.	66	do.	do.,	Murder, . . .	2. 12. 70	To be confined during the pleasure of H. E. the Lord Lieutenant.	3. 10. 70	18
						KILMAINHAM.				
T. M.,	774	M.	41	R.W.	Blacksmith,	Obstructing thoroughfare,	—	—	6. 4. 68	19
M. J.,	1184	M.	60	do.	Labourer,	Larceny, . . .	—	—	16. 4. 68	20
J. C.,	770	M.	17	do.	do.,	do., . . .	4. 4. 68	3 c. mths. h.l.,	4. 4. 68	21
						LIMERICK (Male).				
T. B.,	5	M.	12	R.W.	Cooper,	Cattle stealing, . .	—	Fat trial, . . .	4. 1. 68	19
S—,	—	—	—	—	—	do., . .	4. 7. 68	10 days imp., . .	4. 1. 68	23
J. M.,	642	M.	21	do.	Messenger,	Drunkenness (2 cases), .	11. 7. 68	1 mth. imp. II. do.	11. 7. 68	72
J F K.,	197	M.	31	do.	Farmer,	Murder, . . .	4. 4. 68	To be kept in custody till pleasure of Lord Lieutenant be known	4. 12. 68	16
						LIMERICK (Female).				
M. C.,	244	F.	41	R.W.	Prostitute,	Drunk, . . .	22. 7. 67	6 mths. bail, . .	20. 1. 67	16
L. L.,	577	F.	27	do.	Shoemaker,	Drunk and disorderly, .	11. 8. 10	1 c. mth. h.l., .	11. 1. 10	12
M C.,	474	F.	26	do.	Prostitute,	do., do.	1. 11. 71	1 mth. imprt. . .	1. 11. 71	14

and CONVICT PRISONS, during Year ended 31st December, 1898—*continued.*

No.	Mental Condition on Reception into a Local Prison.	Whether previously Insane.	Length of Imprisonment provious to first symptoms of Insanity (in cases originating in Prison).	Form of Insanity.	Supposed cause of Insanity.	Recovered	Removed to Asylum. Name of Asylum and Date of Removal.	Died in Prison with Date.	Remaining in Prison
				GALWAY.					
9	Insane	Yes	—	Mania	Unknown	—	Ballinasloe, 17. 5. 98.	—	—
10	do.	Unknown	—	Melancholia	do.	—	Ballinasloe, 22. 4. 98.	—	—
11	do.	Yes	—	Mania	Alcoholism	—	Ballinasloe, 8. 7. 98.	—	—
12	do.	Unknown	—	do.	Unknown	—	Ballinasloe, 19. 8. 98.	—	—
13	do.	do.	—	Acute dementia	Probably drink and injury to spine.	—	Ballinasloe, 8. 12. 98.	—	—
				KILKENNY.					
14	Sane	Not known	1 month and 27 days	Mania	Not known	—	Kilkenny, 24. 4. 98.	—	—
15	do.	do.	—	Not known	do.	—	Dundrum, 7. 6. 98.	—	—
16	do.	do.	19 days	Mania	do.	—	Kilkenny, 24. 10. 98.	—	—
17	do.	Yes	—	Not known	do.	—	Dundrum, — 10. 98. After Ardilan at Waterford.	—	—
				KILMAINHAM.					
18	Insane	Not known	—	Mania with delusions	Drink	—	Richmond, 9. 6. 98.	—	—
19	do.	do.	—	Dementia	Not known	—	Richmond, 16. 8. 98.	—	—
20	do.	do.	—	Melancholia	do.	—	Richmond, 4. 10. 98.	—	—
				LIMERICK (Male).					
21	Well conducted	No.	3 months	Mania with delusions	Not known	—	Limerick, 11. 8. 98.	—	—
22	do.	do.	—	do. do.	do.	—	Limerick, 14. 7. 98.	—	—
23	Insane	—	—	Dementia & epileptic	do.	—	Limerick, 8. 6. 98.	—	—
24	do.	No.	—	Impulsive mania, with	do.	—	Dundrum,	—	—

TABLE XIII.—PARTICULARS of each case of INSANITY (amongst Prisoners) in LOCAL

Initials of Name.	Reg. No.	Age		Education	Occupation previous to Conviction.	Crime in Charge.	Date of Conviction (if Convicted).	Sentence (if sentenced).	Date of Reception into a Local Prison.	No.

LONDONDERRY.

MOUNTJOY (Male).

MOUNTJOY (Female).

SLIGO.

arsons, during Year ended 31st December, 1898—*continued.*

Whether previously insane.	Length of Imprisonment previous to first symptom of Insanity (in cases originating in Prison).	Form of Insanity.	Supposed cause of Insanity.	Recovered	Discharged to Prison	Termination of Case. Removed to Asylum. Name of Asylum and Date of Removal.	Died in Prison with Date.	Remaining under Treatment.
LONDONDERRY.								
Yes	—	Chronic mania	Not known		=	Dundrum, 1d. 2. yd.	-	-
do.	—	Acute mania	do.		-	Dundrum, 23. 7. 98.	-	-
No	—	do.	do.		=	Dundrum, 23. 11. 98.	-	-
Yes	4 weeks	Recurrent mania	do.		-	Londonderry, 16. 11 98	-	-
MOUNTJOY (Male).								
Believed to have been. Not known.	—	Recurrent mania	Not known		-	Richmond, 6. 9 98.	-	-
"	—	Mania	do.		-	Richmond, 8 4. 98	-	-
do.	—	Imbecile	Alcohol		-	Richmond, 11. 4. 98.	-	-
do.	60 days	Dementia	Epilepsy		-	Richmond, 27. 4. 98.	-	-
do.	20 days	Acute mania	Epilepsy		-	Richmond, 1. 7. 98	-	-
do.	—	Dementia	Alcoholism		-	Richmond, 1. 7. 98.	-	-
Yes	—	do.	Not known		-	Richmond, 9. 7. 98.	-	-
Not known	—	do.	Alcoholism		-	Richmond, 25. 7. 98.	-	-
do.	—	do.	Not known		-	Richmond, 4. 8. 98.	-	-
Yes	—	do.	do.		-	Richmond, 17. 9 98.	-	-
Not known	—	do.	do.		-	Richmond, 12. 11. 98.	-	-
do.	25 days	do.	do.		-	Kilkenny, 21. 11 98.	-	-
do.	—	Suicidal mania	do.		-	—	-	Yes
MOUNTJOY (Female).								
Not known	—	Mania	Unknown		-	Richmond, 7. 1. 98.	-	-
do.	—	do.	do.		-	Richmond, 9. 2. 98.	-	-
Yes	—	Acute mania	Alcoholism		-	Richmond, 8 4. 98.	-	-
Not known	6 weeks	Dementia	Unknown		-	Richmond, 22. 7. 98.	-	-
do.	—	Acute mania	do.		-	Richmond, 29. 7. 98.	-	-
do.	—	Epilepsy	do.		-	Richmond, 1. 12. 98	-	-

TABLE XIII.—PARTICULARS of each case of INSANITY (amongst Prisoners) in LOCAL

Initials of Name.	Reg. No.	Sex	Age at Entry (Years).	Education.	Comprehension previous to Conviction.	Crime or Charge.	Date of Conviction (if Convicted).	Sentence (if sentenced).	Date of Entry into said Local Prison.	No.

TRALEE.

TULLAMORE.

WATERFORD.

WEXFORD.

CARRICK-ON-SHANNON.   (Minor

DROGHEDA.

ENNISKILLEN.

MULLINGAR.

OMAGH.

WICKLOW.

MARYBOROUGH.   CONVICT

MOUNTJOY.

MOUNTJOY (Female).

aud Convict Prisons, during Year ended 31st December, 1898 *—continued.*

Mental Condition on Reception into Local Prison.	Whether previously Insane.	Length of Imprisonment (previous to first symptoms of Insanity, in cases originating in Prison).	Form of Insanity.	Supposed cause of Insanity.	Termination of Cases.		
					Removed to Asylum. Name of Asylum and Date of Removal.	Died in Prison, with Date.	Still in Prison.
			TRALEE.				
67 Insane.	Yes.	—	—	Not known.	I. Killarney. 16. 7. 97. II. Dundrum. 11. 2. 98.	—	—
			TULLAMORE.				
1 Normal.	Not known.	One month.	General paralysis of the insane.	Not known.	Maryborough, 14. 8. 98	—	—
2 Insane.	Yes.	Insane on committal.	Mania with delusions.	do.	Maryborough, 5. 11. 98.	—	—
			WATERFORD.				
3 Apparently sane.	Not known.	10 days.	Melancholia.	Not known.	Waterford, 23. 2. 98.	—	—
71 do.	No.	81 days.	Religious mania.	do.	Waterford, 17. 5. 98.	—	—
71 Insane.	Yes.	—	Acute mania.	Drink.	Waterford, 98. 11. 98.	—	—
12 do.	No.	—	Melancholia.	Not known.	Dundrum, 17. 11. 98.	—	—
14 Imbecile.	Yes.	—	Imbecility.	Drink.	Dundrum, 13. 13. 98.	—	—
			WEXFORD.				
13 Insane.	Yes.	—	Impulsive.	Defective brain — deaf mute.	Enniscorthy, 29. 8. 96. Enniscorthy back, 11. 7. 98. Dundrum, 27. 7. 98.	—	—
75 do.	do.	—	Mania.	Not known.	Enniscorthy, 12. 8. 98.	—	—
Prisons.)			**CARRICK-ON-SHANNON.**				
	—	—	—	—	—	—	—
	—	—	—	—	—	—	—
			DROGHEDA.				
—	—	—	—	—	—	—	—
			ENNISKILLEN.				
77 Insane.	No.	—	Mania.	Not known.	—	—	Yes
			MULLINGAR.				
78 Insane.	Yes.	—	Senile dementia.	Not known.	Mullingar, 18. 2. 98.	✓	—
			OMAGH.				
79 Insane.	Yes.	—	Mania and delusions.	Not known.	Omagh, 8. 11. 98.	—	—
			WICKLOW.				
—	—	—	—	—	—	—	—
PRISONS.			**MARYBOROUGH.**				
80 Good.	No record.	24 years.	Mania.	Hereditary.	Dundrum, 13. 12. 98.	—	—
			MOUNTJOY.				
81 Sane.	No record.	6 years and 10 months.	Mania.	Not known.	Dundrum, 73. 1. 98.	—	—
82 do.	do.	24 months.	Acute mania.	do.	Dundrum, 18. 3. 98.	—	—
83 do.	do.	1 year.	Mania.	do.	Dundrum, 76. 12. 98.	—	—
84 do.	do.	11 months.	Delusional insanity.	do.	Dundrum, 70. 12. 98.	—	—
—	—	—	**MOUNTJOY (Female).**				

Table XIV.—Return of Restraints, Prison Offences, and Punishments

(As required by section 15

(See paragraph 93 of Report

Prison	Number of Cases of Restraints		Prison Punishments						(a) Total number of Prisoners punished	
	Irons (Handcuffs)	Muffs with Straps or Restraint Jackets	Punishment Cells		Dietary Punishment		Loss of Marks Class or Privileges			
			M.	F.	M.	F.	M.	F.	M.	F.
Total M. & F.	18	108	126		5,557		632		2,739	
Larger Local Prisons.	M.	F.	M.	F.	M.	F.	M.	F.	M.	F.
Armagh,	-	-	3	1	9	8	216	57	16	2	191	34
Belfast,	-	-	4	1	5	-	277	125	8	3	202	109
Castlebar,	-	-	-	2	-	-	74	19	11	1	44	14
Clonmel,	-	-	3	-	9	-	185	-	60	-	117	-
Cork { Local Prisoners. Male, { Convicts,	-	-	3	-	8	-	634	-	90	-	239	-
Cork Female,	-	-	-	7	-	-	-	126	-	8	-	104
Dundalk,	-	-	3	-	7	-	74	-	53	-	76	-
Galway,	1	-	2	1	3	-	46	5	10	-	34	5
Kilkenny,	-	-	4	-	5	-	167	-	112	-	157	-
Kilmainham,	-	-	2	-	2	-	254	-	44	-	244	-
Limerick Male,	-	-	4	-	-	-	643	-	13	-	258	-
Limerick Female,	-	-	-	3	-	8	-	32	-	6	-	82
Londonderry,	-	-	3	3	1	-	144	18	3	-	123	14
Maryboro',	-	-	11	-	6	-	139	-	44	-	141	-
Mountjoy Female,	-	-	-	15	-	5	-	22	-	6	-	18
Sligo,	-	-	2	-	4	1	170	2	53	-	129	3
Tralee,	-	-	-	-	-	-	201	5	12	1	116	2
Tullamore,	-	-	2	-	-	-	201	6	23	1	131	6
Waterford,	-	-	-	-	-	1	90	3	7	-	37	4
Wexford,	-	-	1	-	-	-	154	3	13	-	88	3
Minor Prisons										
Carrick-on-Shannon	-	-	-	-	-	-	-	-	-	-	-	-
Drogheda,	-	-	-	-	-	-	-	-	-	-	-	-
Kilmallock,	-	-	1	-	-	-	-	-	-	-	-	-
Mullingar,	-	-	-	-	-	-	-	-	-	-	-	-
Omagh,	-	-	-	-	-	-	1	-	-	-	1	-
Wicklow,	-	-	-	-	-	-	5	-	-	-	5	-
Total Local Prisons	1	-	51	36	51	18	2,945	425	564	17	2,525	319
Convict Prisons.										
Maryborough,	-	-	1	-	58	-	29	-	1	-	10	-
Mountjoy,	11	-	17	-	19	-	111	-	26	-	61	-
Mountjoy Female,	-	-	-	5	-	3	-	6	-	1	-	5
Total Convict Prisons.	11	-	18	5	68	3	137	6	31	1	100	5
Grand Total,	18	-	69	39	109	21	3,157	450	596	18	2,488	364

* Besides this there was one punishment inflicted in New Ross Bridewell.
† These totals do not agree with the total prison population, &c., in consequence of transfers and appeals appendix

In LOCAL and CONVICT PRISONS from 1st JANUARY, 1898, to 31st DECEMBER, 1898.

of 40 & 41 Vict., cap. 49.)

of Royal Commission, 1884.)

Number of Prisoners not punished.		Total number of Prisoners during the Year. (Columns a & b)		Prison Offences.										Prisons.
				Violence.		Escapes and Attempts to Escape.		Idleness.		Other Breaches of Regulations.		Total Offences.		
M.	F.	M.	F.	M.	F.	M.	F.	M.	F.	M.	F.	M.	F.	
65,159		49,970		195		8		9,450		5,958		6,648		Total M. & F.
														Larger Local Prisons
111	391	495	817	7	6	—	—	239	49	105	17	841	78	Armagh.
3,791	2,500	5,291	2,498	2	—	—	—	104	125	196	34	804	167	Belfast.
246	181	401	153	—	—	—	—	72	8	98	37	130	29	Cavlebar.
316	—	642	—	7	—	—	—	281	—	197	—	477	—	Clonmel.
1,194	—	2,409	—	8	—	—	—	195	—	541	—	744	—	Local Prisoners. } Cork
18	—	18	—	—	—	—	—	—	—	2	—	2	—	Convicts. } Male.
—	1,298	—	1,362	—	7	—	—	—	7	—	377	—	168	Cork Female.
779	—	675	—	1	—	—	—	53	—	214	—	266	—	Dundalk.
641	107	698	203	8	—	—	—	14	—	60	7	71	1	Galway.
621	—	1,027	—	6	—	—	—	16	—	281	—	307	—	Kilkenny.
8,164	—	3,410	—	6	—	—	—	163	—	419	—	608	—	Kilmainham.
1,220	—	1,480	—	8	—	—	—	247	—	826	—	610	—	Limerick Male.
—	654	—	588	—	11	—	—	—	—	—	40	—	51	Limerick Female.
1,154	680	1,975	576	7	—	—	—	44	1	111	18	165	19	Londonderry.
3,290	—	5,420	—	10	—	—	—	701	—	179	—	290	—	Mountjoy.
—	6,996	—	6,404	—	11	—	—	—	—	—	20	—	81	Mountjoy Female.
451	802	691	300	1	—	—	—	137	—	165	8	328	8	Sligo.
696	158	713	162	—	—	—	—	206	8	91	6	297	6	Tralee.
647	270	738	806	—	—	—	—	178	1	377	11	656	19	Tullamore.
107	103	834	487	1	2	—	—	85	1	56	8	62	12	Waterford.
574	119	474	129	3	—	—	—	110	—	120	4	256	1	Wexford.
														Minor Prisons.
194	64	124	84	—	—	—	—	—	—	—	—	—	—	Carrick-on-Shannon.
273	61	273	81	—	—	—	—	—	—	—	—	—	—	Drogheda.
181	87	181	27	—	—	—	—	—	—	—	—	—	—	Enniskillen.
147	85	247	80	—	—	—	—	—	—	—	—	—	—	Mullingar.
441	80	355	80	—	—	—	—	1	—	—	—	1	—	Omagh.
115	23	150	23	—	—	—	—	2	—	4	—	6	—	Wicklow.

TABLE XV. —OFFENCES and COMMITMENTS of JUVENILES, i.e., PRISONERS under 16 years of age, from 1st January, 1898, to 31st December, 1898 (Included in foregoing Tables).

Prisons.	At Assizes and Quarter Sessions.	Summarily.	Committed for Trial.	Total Convicted.	Not Convicted and Untried.	Total Number of Commitments.
TOTAL, M. & F.	- 18	19	190	- 19	809	19	40	31	289

MALES.

Larger Prisons.									
Armagh,	-	-	1	6	-	1	6	1	6	1
Belfast,	-	-	9	17	-	2	17	-	15	22
Castlebar,	-	-	-	7	-	-	1	-	1	1
Clonmel,	-	-	2	9	-	1	1	-	1	3
Cork Male,	-	-	1	21	-	2	22	-	6	26
Dundalk,	-	1	-	6	-	-	6	-	1	1
Galway,	-	-	-	6	-	-	6	2	7	7
Kilkenny,	-	-	-	1	-	-	1	-	1	1
Kilmainham,	-	1	1	25	-	1	11	-	60	60
Limerick Male,	-	-	-	6	-	-	6	-	1	1
Londonderry,	-	2	-	6	-	-	11	-	1	11
Mountjoy,	-	1	1	43	-	1	43	-	6	11
Sligo,	-	1	-	3	-	-	1	-	1	1
Tralee,	-	-	1	6	-	1	6	-	1	1
Tullamore,	-	-	1	5	-	1	6	-	1	6
Waterford,	-	-	-	11	-	-	11	1	-	3	11
Wexford,	-	-	-	6	-	-	1	-	1	1
Minor Prisons.									
Carrick-on-Shannon,	-	-	-	1	-	-	1	-	1	1
Drogheda,								2		1
Enniskillen,	-	-	-	1	-	-	1	-	1	1
Mullingar,	-	-	-	-	-	-	-	3	1	1
Omagh,	-	-	1	-	-	-	-	-	-	1
Wicklow,	-	-	-	-	-	-	1	-	1	1
Total Males,	-	18	19	197	-	19	180	11	67	30	247

FEMALES.

Larger Prisons.									
Armagh,	-	-	-	6	-	-	2	-	1	6
Belfast,	-	-	-	5	-	-	3	-	1	4
Castlebar,	-	-	-	1	-	-	-	-	-	-
Cork Female,	-	-	-	6	-	-	1	-	1	6
Galway,	-	-	-	1	-	-	1	-	1	1
Limerick Female,	-	-	-	1	-	-	1	1	-	1
Londonderry,	-	-	-	1	-	-	1	-	1	1
Mountjoy Female,	-	-	-	6	-	-	6	-	1	7
Sligo,	-	-	-	1	-	-	-	-	-	-
Tralee,	-	-	-	1	-	-	1	-	-	1
Tullamore,	-	-	-	-	-	-	-	-	-	-
Waterford,	-	-	-	3	-	-	6	-	1	6
Wexford,	-	-	-	-	-	-	-	-	-	-
Minor Prisons.									
Carrick-on-Shannon,	-	-	-	-	-	-	-	2	-	1
Drogheda,	-	-	-	-	-	-	-	-	-	-
Enniskillen,	-	-	-	-	-	-	-	-	-	-
Mullingar,	-	-	-	1	-	-	2	-	-	1
Omagh,	-	-	-	-	-	-	-	-	-	-
Wicklow,	-	-	-	-	-	-	-	-	-	-
Total Females,	-	-	-	63	-	-	62	1	16	1	60

TABLE XVI.—SENTENCES on JUVENILE PRISONERS COMMITTED from the 1st January, 1898, to 31st December, 1898.

Prisons.																			Total
TOTAL, M. & F.	-	-	-	-	-	3	-	9	88	47	61	3	4	-	18	96	11	252

MALES.

Larger Prisons.																			
Armagh,	-	-	-	-	-	-	-	1	1	1	1	-	4	-	-	-	1	4
Belfast,	-	-	-	-	-	-	-	4	4	8	1	-	4	-	-	2	-	19
Castlebar,	-	-	-	-	-	-	-	-	-	-	3	-	-	-	-	-	-	7
Clonmel,	-	-	-	-	-	-	1	3	1	5	-	-	-	-	-	-	6	24
Cork Male,	-	-	-	-	-	-	-	4	3	8	1	-	-	-	-	1	6	
Dundalk,	-	-	-	-	-	-	-	-	-	1	-	-	-	-	-	1	-	2
Galway,	-	-	-	-	-	-	-	1	9	1	-	-	-	-	-	-	-	4
Kilkenny,	-	-	-	-	-	-	-	-	-	-	1	-	-	-	-	-	-	1
Maryborough,	-	-	-	-	-	-	-	1	2	1	-	-	-	11	11	8	23
Limerick Male,	-	-	-	-	-	-	2	4	1	-	-	-	-	-	-	9
Londonderry,	-	-	-	-	2	-	1	7	7	-	-	-	-	-	-	13
Mullingar,	-	-	-	-	-	-	8	16	76	-	-	-	-	-	-	48
Sligo,	-	-	-	-	-	-	2	-	-	-	-	-	-	-	-	4
Tralee,	-	-	-	-	-	-	1	7	2	-	-	-	1	8	-	10
Kilmore,	-	-	-	-	-	-	-	-	1	-	-	-	-	-	-	4
Waterford,	-	-	-	-	-	-	-	1	10	-	-	-	-	-	-	11
Wexford,	-	-	-	-	-	-	-	1	1	1	-	-	-	-	-	3
Minor Prisons.																		
Carrick-on-Shan.,	-	-	-	-	-	-	-	-	-	-	-	-	-	-	-	-
Drogheda,	-	-	-	-	-	-	-	-	-	1	-	-	-	-	-	1
Dundalk,	-	-	-	-	-	-	-	-	2	-	-	-	-	-	2
Kilkenny,	-	-	-	-	-	-	-	-	-	-	-	-	-	-	-
Omagh,	-	-	-	-	-	-	-	-	-	-	-	-	-	-	-
Wicklow,	-	-	-	-	-	-	-	-	-	-	-	-	-	-	-
Total Males,	-	-	-	-	-	3	-	3	88	48	66	1	4	-	18	88	11	199

FEMALES.

Larger Prisons.																			
Armagh,	-	-	-	-	-	-	-	1	-	1	-	-	-	-	2
Belfast,	-	-	-	-	-	-	-	-	-	-	-	-	1	-	6
Castlebar,	-	-	-	-	-	-	-	-	-	-	-	-	-	-	-
Cork Female,	-	-	-	-	-	-	-	-	1	-	-	-	-	-	1
Galway,	-	-	-	-	-	-	-	-	1	-	-	-	-	-	1
Limerick Female,	-	-	-	-	-	-	-	-	1	-	-	-	-	-	1
Londonderry,	-	-	-	-	-	-	-	-	-	-	-	-	-	-	-
Mountjoy Female,	-	-	-	-	-	-	1	7	-	-	-	-	-	-	8
Sligo,	-	-	-	-	-	-	-	1	-	-	-	-	-	-	1
Tralee,	-	-	-	-	-	-	-	-	-	-	-	-	-	-	-
Kilmore,	-	-	-	-	-	-	1	-	-	-	-	-	-	-	1
Waterford,	-	-	-	-	-	-	-	1	2	-	-	-	-	-	3
Wexford,	-	-	-	-	-	-	-	-	-	-	-	-	-	-	-
Minor Prisons.																		
Carrick-on-Shan.,	-	-	-	-	-	-	-	-	-	-	-	-	-	-	-
Drogheda,	-	-	-	-	-	-	-	-	-	-	-	-	-	-	-
Enniskillen,	-	-	-	-	-	-	-	-	-	-	-	-	-	-	-
Kilkenny,	-	-	-	-	-	-	-	-	2	-	-	-	-	-	2
Omagh,	-	-	-	-	-	-	-	-	-	-	-	-	-	-	-
Wicklow,	-	-	-	-	-	-	-	-	-	-	-	-	-	-	-
Total Females,	-	-	-	-	-	1	-	-	9	1	18	8	-	-	-	8	-	53

TABLE XVII.—CONDITION of JUVENILES as to

Prisons.	EDUCATION ON COMMITTAL.							
	Neither Read nor Write.		Read or Read and Write Imperfectly.		Read and Write Well.		Superior Instruction.	
	Under 12 years.	12 and under 16 years.	Under 12 years.	12 and under 16 years.	Under 12 years.	12 and under 16 years.	Under 12 years.	12 and under 16 years.
Total, M. & F., . .	10	89	10	108	11	93	–	5

MALES.

Armagh, ...	–	8	1	1	1	8	–	–
Belfast, ...	1	4	1	12	–	11	–	–
Castlebar, . . .	–	1	–	–	–	8	–	–
Clonmel, ...	–	–	1	1	1	8	–	–
Cork, Male, . . .	1	4	1	18	1	11	–	–
Dundalk, . . .	–	1	–	5	–	5	–	–
Galway, . . .	–	2	–	2	1	1	–	–
Kilkenny, . . .	–	2	–	1	–	4	–	–
Kilmainham, . .	2	11	2	80	–	11	–	4
Limerick, Male, .	–	2	–	7	–	4	–	–
Londonderry, . .	–	1	–	8	–	2	–	–
Mountjoy, . . .	4	17	1	10	1	14	–	–
Sligo, ...	–	–	–	8	–	1	–	–
Tralee, ...	–	3	–	1	2	4	–	–
Tullamore, . . .	–	2	–	1	–	3	–	–
Waterford, . . .	2	2	–	6	–	–	–	–
Wexford, . . .	–	1	–	1	–	–	–	–
Minor Prisons.								
Carrick-on-Shannon, .	–	–	–	–	–	–	–	–
Drogheda, . . .	–	1	–	1	–	–	–	–
Enniskillen, . .	–	1	–	1	–	–	–	–
Mullingar, . . .	–	–	1	1	–	–	–	–
Omagh, . . .	–	–	–	–	–	–	–	–
Wicklow, . . .	–	–	1	–	–	–	–	–
Total Males, . .	10	74	10	93	10	76	–	5

FEMALES.

Armagh, ...	–	1	–	1	–	7	–	–
Belfast, ...	–	–	–	–	–	7	–	–
Castlebar, . . .	–	–	–	–	–	–	–	–
Cork Female, . .	–	–	–	–	1	4	–	–
Galway, . . .	–	1	–	–	–	1	–	–
Limerick, Female, .	–	–	–	1	–	1	–	–
Londonderry, . .	–	–	–	–	–	–	–	–
Mountjoy, Female, .	–	1	–	1	–	1	–	–
Sligo, ...	–	1	–	1	–	–	–	–
Tralee, ...	–	–	–	–	–	–	–	–
Tullamore, . . .	–	–	–	–	–	–	–	–
Waterford, . . .	–	1	–	1	–	–	–	–
Wexford, . . .	–	1	–	1	–	–	–	–
Minor Prisons.								
Carrick-on-Shannon, .	–	–	–	–	–	–	–	–
Drogheda, . . .	–	–	–	1	–	–	–	–
Enniskillen, . .	–	–	–	–	–	–	–	–
Mullingar, . . .	–	1	–	1	–	–	–	–
Omagh, . . .	–	–	–	–	–	–	–	–
Wicklow, . . .	–	–	–	–	–	–	–	–
Total Females, . .	–	8	–	11	1	17	–	–

Education and Religion in 1898.

Religion.											Prisons.
Protestant Episcopalians of Ireland.		Presbyterians.		Roman Catholics.		Other Religions.		Total.			
Under 18 years.	18 and under 16 years.	Under 18 years.	18 and under 16 years.	Under 18 years.	18 and under 16 years.	Under 18 years.	18 and under 16 years.	Under 18 years.	18 and under 16 years.		
1	17	1	16	29	260	-	-	51	853		Total, M. & F.

MALES.

1	9	2	10	1	9	-	-	7	9		Armagh.
-	10	-	-	-	12	-	-	9	42		Belfast.
-	-	-	-	-	9	-	-	-	5		Castlebar.
-	-	-	-	1	9	-	-	1	9		Clonmel.
-	-	-	-	5	79	-	-	5	79		Cork, Male
-	-	-	-	-	6	-	-	1	6		Dundalk.
-	-	-	-	2	7	-	-	1	7		Galway.
-	-	-	-	-	1	-	-	1	1		Kilkenny.
-	2	-	-	4	57	-	-	4	59		Kilmainham.
-	-	-	-	-	9	-	-	-	9		Limerick, Male.
-	1	-	4	-	9	-	-	-	11		Londonderry.
-	-	-	-	4	41	-	-	5	41		Mountjoy.
-	-	-	-	-	6	-	-	-	6		Sligo.
-	-	-	-	2	6	-	-	2	9		Tralee.
-	-	-	-	-	6	-	-	-	6		Tullamore.
-	-	-	-	2	11	-	-	7	11		Waterford.
-	-	-	-	-	9	-	-	-	6		Wexford.
											Minor Prisons.
-	-	-	-	-	-	-	-	-	-		Carrick-on-Shan.
-	1	-	-	-	2	-	-	-	2		Drogheda.
-	1	-	-	-	2	-	-	-	2		Enniskillen.
-	-	-	-	2	1	-	-	2	1		Mullingar.
-	-	-	-	-	1	-	-	-	1		Omagh.
-	-	-	-	1	1	-	-	1	1		Wicklow.
1	17	1	14	27	216	-	-	30	347		**Total Males.**

FEMALES.

-	-	-	1	-	2	-	-	-	3		Armagh.
-	-	-	-	-	6	-	-	-	6		Belfast.
-	-	-	-	-	-	-	-	-	-		Cavtlobar.
-	-	-	-	1	4	-	-	1	6		Cork, Female.
-	-	-	-	-	4	-	-	-	6		Galway.
-	-	-	-	-	1	-	-	-	1		Limerick, Female.
-	-	-	-	-	1	-	-	-	1		Londonderry.
-	-	-	-	-	9	-	-	-	9		Mountjoy, Female.
-	-	-	-	-	9	-	-	-	9		Sligo.
-	-	-	-	-	1	-	-	-	1		Tralee.
-	-	-	-	-	1	-	-	-	1		Tullamore.
-	-	-	-	-	4	-	-	-	4		Waterford.
-	-	-	-	-	-	-	-	-	-		Wexford.
											Minor Prisons.
-	-	-	-	-	-	-	-	-	-		Carrick-on-Shan.
-	-	-	-	-	1	-	-	-	1		Drogheda.
-	-	-	-	-	-	-	-	-	-		Enniskillen.
-	-	-	-	-	2	-	-	-	2		Mullingar.
-	-	-	-	-	-	-	-	-	-		Omagh.
-	-	-	-	-	-	-	-	-	-		Wicklow.
-	-	-	2	1	64	-	-	1	36		**Total Females.**

TABLE XVIII.—CRIMES of CONVICTS committed under fresh sentences of penal servitude during the year ended 31st December, 1898, and of all Convicts in custody on that date.

Crime.	Number Cases allured under fresh sentences of penal servitude during year.		No. in custody on 31st Dec., 1898					
			Maryborough					Mountjoy Female
	M.	F.	Invalids	Intermediate and others	Mountjoy	Total Males	
	M.	F.	M.	M.	M.	M.	F.
Accessory after the fact to Murder,	—	—	—	1	—	1	—
Administering Poison with intent,	—	—	—	1	1	1	—
Arson,	2	—	—	1	2	3	—
Assault, Bodily Harm,	—	—	—	—	3	3	—
Assault and Robbery,	8	—	—	1	7	8	—
Assault with intent to Murder,	1	—	—	—	3	3	—
Attempt to steal,	—	—	—	1	1	1	—
Attempt to blow up House,	—	—	—	1	1	1	—
Attempt to Murder,	—	—	—	6	1	1	—
Attempt to fire at with intent,	—	—	—	1	1	1	—
Attempt to set fire to Dwelling-house,	1	—	—	—	1	2	—
Base Coin, Having, making, uttering, or intending to utter,	—	—	—	1	6	2	—
Bigamy,	—	—	—	—	—	3	—
Breaking and Entering,	—	—	—	—	—	3	—
Burglary,	3	—	1	6	11	18	—
Carnal knowledge of Girl under 13,	1	—	—	1	5	6	—
Cattle Stealing,	1	—	—	1	3	4	—
Conspiracy to Murder,	—	—	1	1	1	1	—
Conspiracy to Defraud,	—	—	—	1	—	1	—
Felony,	—	—	—	1	6	7	—
Feloniously entering Dwelling-house,	—	—	1	—	—	1	—
Forgery,	1	—	—	2	2	4	—
Having Implements of Housebreaking,	—	—	—	1	—	1	—
Highway Robbery,	1	—	—	1	3	3	—
Housebreaking,	11	—	—	6	46	62	—
Larceny from Person,	—	—	1	1	2	4	2
Larceny, &c.	51	3	1	15	40	59	6
Malicious burning,	—	1	—	—	1	1	1
Malicious Wounding,	—	1	—	—	1	—	1
Manslaughter,	7	3	6	16	24	43	4
Military Offences,	1	—	—	—	4	4	—
Murder,	8	—	3	2	19	22	8
Obstructing Railway,	—	—	—	1	—	1	—
Obtaining Goods and Money by False Pretences,	8	—	—	—	5	5	—
Rape,	6	—	—	8	13	21	—
Rape and aiding,	—	—	—	8	—	8	—
Receiving and previous conviction,	3	—	—	1	6	8	—
Feloniously damaging Dwelling-house,	1	—	—	—	7	7	—
Robbery,	—	—	—	4	1	6	—
Sheep stealing,	2	—	—	—	6	7	—
Sodomy,	—	—	—	1	6	7	—
Throwing Vitriol, with Intent,	—	—	—	—	1	1	—
Whisky Offence,	1	—	—	1	8	8	—
Wounding,	—	—	—	—	1	1	—
Wounding with Intent,	1	—	—	1	8	8	—
Wounding and grievous bodily harm,	5	—	—	1	8	6	—
Totals,	94	8	8	96	308	312	19

TABLE XIX. —STATEMENT of ACCOMMODATION for PRISONERS in the Local and
Convict Prisons (not including Minor Prisons and Bridewells), and of the daily
average and greatest number of Male and Female Prisoners, respectively, during
the year ended 31st December, 1898.

	Number of Cells first government			Number of other Cells that could be made available.			Number of Rooms.			Daily Average Number of Prisoners.			Greatest Number of Prisoners.	
	Males	Females	Total	Males	Females	Total	Males	Females	Total	Males	Females	Total	Males	Females
Larger Local Prisons.														
Armagh	71	49	120	–	–	–	7	1	8	61	18	79	83	89
Belfast	383	151	535	98	2	100	6	3	9	544	112	656	605	149
Castlebar	45	16	61	–	–	–	3	2	4	76	8	32	41	15
Clonmel	161	–	161	–	–	–	4	–	4	78	–	78	144	–
Cork, Male	263	–	263	–	–	–	3	–	3	321	–	321	328	–
Cork, Female	–	146	155	–	–	–	–	6	8	–	61	61	–	119
Dundalk	162	–	162	–	–	–	3	–	8	86	–	96	112	–
Galway	90	19	162	8	8	16	2	1	4	77	16	93	102	25
Kilkenny	169	8	177	8	–	3	2	–	2	122	–	132	171	–
Kilmainham	149	–	149	–	–	–	12	–	12	144	–	144	208	–
Limerick, Male	124	–	124	–	–	–	8	–	2	96	–	95	167	–
Limerick, Female	–	57	57	–	5	5	–	1	1	–	51	41	–	49
Londonderry	169	29	128	–	–	–	3	3	6	149	20	157	165	49
Sligo	85	25	112	–	–	–	2	3	5	67	15	73	35	14
Tralee	75	14	89	–	–	–	4	1	5	99	9	98	62	18
Tullamore	89	39	129	5	–	5	19	2	21	71	16	87	81	19
Waterford	73	40	112	1	–	1	4	2	6	85	9	95	85	42
Wexford	66	51	117	–	–	–	7	1	3	44	7	51	71	17
Convict Prison.														
Maryborough	114	–	114	3	–	8	–	–	–	106	–	106	110	–
Local and Convict Prison.														
Mountjoy	497	377	876	95	–	95	–	5	5	444	305	759	584	398
TOTAL	3735	1496	5531	40	14	99	77	77	144	1900	670	2585	–	–

a

during the Year 1898.

Number others remained.		Total number of Prisoners remained.	
M.	F.	M.	F.
.	.	11	10

TABLE XXI.—RETURN of the STAFF of the undermentioned PRISONS and BRIDEWELLS on 31st December, 1898, including vacancies

PRISONS	MALE OFFICERS							FEMALE OFFICERS					TOTAL	
	Governors and Deputy Chairs	Chief Warders	Chaplains	Surgeons & Assistants	Clerical and Store Keepers	Warders and Principal Warders	Other School Gate Officers	Matron and Deputy Superintendent	Matrons	Warders and Assistant Matrons	Servants	Male	Female
LARGER LOCAL PRISONS													
Armagh,	1	1	1	3	1	11	7	—	—	1	3	20	5
Belfast,	2	1	1	3	1	31	—	—	1	14	2	41	14
Castlebar,	1	1	1	2	1	5	—	—	—	2	—	12	—
Clonmel,	1	1	1	2	1	11	—	—	—	—	—	12	—
Cork, Male,	1	1	1	6	1	17	—	—	—	—	1	24	—
Cork, Female,	—	1	1	—	—	—	—	—	—	16	1	—	14
Dundalk,	1	1	1	4	1	11	—	—	—	—	1	10	1
Galway,	1	1	1	2	1	8	—	—	—	2	1	14	3
Kilkenny,	1	1	1	2	1	14	—	—	—	—	1	20	3
Kilmainham,	2	1	1	2	1	15	—	—	—	—	1	24	3
Limerick, Male,	1	1	1	2	1	16	—	—	—	—	1	27	3
Limerick, Female,	—	1	1	2	—	—	—	—	—	7	1	1	3
Londonderry,	1	1	1	2	1	16	1	—	—	2	1	23	3
Sligo,	1	1	1	3	1	10	—	—	—	2	1	16	3
Tralee,	1	1	1	2	1	16	—	—	—	2	1	14	3
Tullamore,	1	1	1	2	1	11	—	—	1	3	1	17	3
Waterford,	1	1	1	2	1	7	—	—	1	3	—	14	3
Wexford,	1	1	1	2	1	7	—	—	—	3	—	14	3
CONVICT PRISONS													
Maryboro',	1	1	7	1	1	25	3	—	—	—	1	17	1
LOCAL AND CONVICT PRISON													
Mountjoy,	2	9	4	6	7	45	20	1	7	71	3	126	81
MINOR PRISONS													
Carrick-on-Shannon,	—	1	—	—	—	1	—	—	1	—	—	3	1
Drogheda,	—	1	—	—	—	1	—	—	1	—	—	3	1
Kanturk,	—	1	—	—	—	1	—	—	1	—	—	3	1
Mullingar,	—	1	—	—	—	1	—	—	1	—	—	3	1
Omagh,	—	1	—	—	—	1	—	—	1	—	—	3	1
Wicklow,	—	1	—	—	—	1	—	—	1	—	—	3	1
LOCK-UP.													
Ennis,	—	1	—	—	—	2	—	—	1	—	—	3	1
BRIDEWELLS													
Ballaghaderreen,	—	1	—	—	—	1	—	—	—	—	—	1	—
Ballina,	—	1	—	—	—	1	—	—	—	—	—	1	—
Bantry,	—	1	—	—	—	1	—	—	—	—	—	1	1
Cahirciveen,	—	1	—	—	—	1	—	—	—	1	—	1	1
Clifden,	—	1	—	—	—	1	—	—	—	1	—	1	1
Fermoy,	—	1	—	—	—	1	—	—	—	—	—	1	1
Kilrush,	—	1	—	—	—	1	—	—	—	1	—	1	1
Loughrea,	—	1	—	—	—	1	—	—	—	1	—	1	1
Milton,	—	1	—	—	—	1	—	—	—	—	—	1	—
New Ross,	—	1	—	—	—	1	—	—	—	1	—	1	1
Nenagh,	—	1	—	—	—	1	—	—	—	1	—	1	1
Parsonstown,	—	1	—	—	—	1	—	—	—	—	—	1	1
Youghal,	—	1	—	—	—	1	—	—	—	1	—	1	1
Total, 1898,	22	54	47	59	21	290	30	1	20	66	21	529	133
Total, 1897,	21	54	42	70	14	244	2	1	14	61	20	340	130

* The increase is accounted for by the fact that the staff of the Convict Prisons is for the first time included in this return.

TABLE XXII.—ESCAPES from PRISONS and BRIDEWELLS from 1st
January, 1898, to 31st December, 1898.

Prisons, &c., from which Escapes were effected.	Initials of Name			Date of escape.	Offence of which convicted or charged.	Trial or Untried.	Whether again found especially or with others.	Whether taken or not
Maryborough,	J. B.,	M.		60 21, 19, 92.	1. Feloniously wounding, II. Burglary, III. Feloniously receiving.	Tried,	With others,	Yes.
Do.,	J. C.,	M.		20 21, 19, 98.	Breaking and entering, also larceny, and previous conviction for felony.	do.,	do.,	do.

TABLE XXIII.—WORKS of RECONSTRUCTION, REPAIRS, &c., by Contract and by
Prison Labour, during the Year ended 31st December, 1898.

LARGER LOCAL PRISONS.

Prisons.	Labour (Contract or Prison).	Detail of Works.
Armagh,	Contract,	Erecting self-contained cart weighbridge; painting front of prison and railings, and warders' cottages; painting walls with mineral, repairing roof, and pavering rooms of one cottage; fitting up electric bell between male hospital ward and central hall, and repairing electric bells.
Do.,	Prison,	Putting extra window in one warder's cottage; fitting front plate to heating apparatus, male wing; putting window in weighbridge house; building pier for new weighbridge; carrying out general carpentry, painting, gazing, plumbing, painting, whitewashing, and general repairs to buildings.
Belfast,	Contract,	Erecting new hospital; fitting up two new heating boilers in A and D wings.
Do.,	Prison,	Completing twenty new stone sheds, and commencing removal of walls surrounding separation exercise yards; altering and renovating single officers' quarters, by converting eight small rooms, and one hospital room, into five dormitories, capable of accommodating twenty men; fitting up lavatory with bath, &c., in connection with same; converting five W.Cs., not required for use, and seven rooms into nineteen extra single cells in male division; breaking out gateway on lower wall at end of D wing and erecting gate on same; carrying drinking water direct to each wing of the prison by laying pipes from main; papering and painting part of Governor's house, and adding three fire grates to same; painting and limewashing the entire prison in accordance with regulations laid down in Circular 458; cleaning and repairing roofs, eaves, spouting, &c.; effecting general repairs to carpentry, plumbing, painting, and glazing work, &c., also to furnaces, ranges, roads, paths, &c.
Clonmel,	Contract,	Flooring new dining room and dormitory; supplying new wire ropes to barrel clock and bell in clock tower; taking down eighteen metal doors in female prison, replacing with new wooden doors; repairing roofs of chapel, officers' quarters, male and female prison.

Table XXIII.—Works of Reconstruction, Repairs, &c.—*continued.*

Prison.	Labour (Contract or Prison).	Detail of Works.
Castlebar.	Prison,	Setting new boiler in range, Governor's house; fitting up dark room; repairing slating and cast-iron gutters; removing chimney pots, front entrance; making new grates and shelves; making window blinds, officers' new quarters; painting, colouring and whitewashing offices, officers' quarters, church, male and female prisons; introducing and distributing town water; sundry repairs to gas and hot water pipes.
Clonmel,	Contract,	Supplying and erecting a hot water tank in hospital bath room; introducing water into officers' new kitchen, and fitting up lavatory in connection with same; painting and papering chief warder's sitting-room. Fixing up three gas chandeliers in paddock and observation cell; repairing chimneys and roofs of Governor's house and R. C. church; re-roofing sitting-room of ward [illegible] vestry of R. C. church; and office W.C.; supplying and erecting new boiler in laundry and supplying new door frames and fire-blocks for same; remodelling storerooms for clothes in laundry; erecting a lath and plaster partition in the top storey of Governor's house, and fitting up a bath, skylight, and W.C. in same; supplying and fitting up flushbacks in ranges and limewashing rooms of the prison entrance; bucking [illegible] of old mortar and re-dashing front wall of prison; repairing casual, pump and general repairs of water pipes, gas cocks, &c.
Do.,	Prison,	Remaking a new execution scaffold; fixing up new door frames and fire-blocks in laundry boiler and furnace; polishing loose slates on roofs of No. 2 prison, Governor's house, and hospital; converting a room at Governor's house; papering two rooms in Governor's house and passage leading to bathroom of same; removing the old Marshal-sea building and the walls around yards of old prison; general repairs in painting, glazing, carpentry, and whitewashing throughout the prison.
Cork, Male.	Contract,	Taking down, cleaning, and re-erecting turret clock in No. 5 section; painting and papering five bedrooms, hall, stairway, &c., of Governor's house; painting entrance gate; erecting a large bell in belfry of chapel; raising and re-setting ridge tiles and repairing slating, &c., No. 10 section; supplying and laying metal hot water heating pipes through three corridors in No. 8 section, and connecting them with existing pipes in an adjoining section.
Do.,	Prison,	Riveting a new grate and gas bracket in Governor's house; making and erecting thirty-seven new window sashes in corridors No. 10 section; repairing lead gutter on roofs of No. 1 and 2 sections; erecting new gate on entrance to rubbish depot, brewer yard; erecting new coal closets on chapel; repairing ovens in bakery; erecting new shelving for prisoners' clothing in hospital; erecting six washing troughs in laundry; painting new furnace bars in steam boiler in prison cook-house; repairing rackets, &c., of wash pump; erecting three W.C.'s and supplying them with water; laying new gas main and supplying cells, &c., with gaslights and bells in No. 9 block; effecting general repairs and minor works of maintenance throughout the prison; the work of reconstruction of No. 9 block has been completed.
Cork Female,	Contract,	Slating roof of cookhouse; repairing the roof of prison; repairing cell bath; repairing the plaster of the walls of store yard; lathing and plastering ceiling of miscellaneous stores, and re-coating large stone and repairing ceiling of front gate; repairing the ranges of the prison; supplying and fixing new grating for tank in field outside prison.
Do.,	Prison,	Making a new door for coal yard; fixing new clothes lines in laundry; repairing coping of wall in wardens' quarters; painting and renovating officers' quarters; whitewashing and painting prison cells, &c.; fixing new supports to roof of wardens' kitchen; fixing new sluice valve in water main; fixing new waste pipes for overtoping water from well to the prison sewers; general repairs to fireplaces, &c., throughout the prison.

TABLE XXIII.—WORKS OF RECONSTRUCTION, REPAIRS, &c.—*continued.*

Prisons.	Labour (Constructed Prison).	Detail of Works.
Dundalk,	Contract,	Repairing crank pump with new wheels, brass pedestals, and beams; repairing steam boiler and water gauge valves; setting new pan in portable boiler in cook house; repairing water pipes.
Do.,	Prison,	Setting new bottom in steam boiler; erecting wire netting over store pipes in laundry; putting in new grate in guard room; erecting potato house on back entrance gate; erecting new cooking stove in cook-house; carrying out general repairs and minor works of maintenance.
Galway,	Contract,	Repairing hot and cold water pipes from boiler in Governor's house; repairing portion of valley on roof of male hospital by removing old lead and replacing it with new lead; putting in new gas cock and repairing gas pipes at entrance gate; repairing hot water pipe to supply cistern No. 3 section male prison; supplying and putting on tap on water pipe in officers' room.
Do.,	Prison,	Repairing roof of male prison, general store, and male hospital; mending and sheeting boilers in Governor's house; making and fixing up shelving in general store; laying new water drain in cement, front of stone sheds, and repairing stone sheds; repairing heating furnace, female prison; repairing and making bottoms for fireplaces of range in cook-house; making bottoms for fireplaces and putting new firebricks in boilers; papering and repairing walls of two bedrooms in chief warder's quarters; putting new grate in kitchen of mess servant's cottage; putting in new hopper head roof of chief warder's quarters and repairing rain water pipe; making and fixing up new window in maintenance general store; carrying out general repairs and minor works of maintenance.
Kilkenny,	Contract,	Changing line of electric bells from underground to overhead from Governor's and chief warder's quarters to hall of prison; general repairs to crank pump, including the supplying of three new working barrels, with rings and valves; erecting a porch at entrance door of Governor's quarters; exchanging existing incandescent gas burners for bye-pass burners; repairing range and grate of Governor's quarters; glazing windows of church with stained glass; repairing of electric bells; re-building of porch at back of Governor's quarters; painting down, windows, all wood and ironwork front of cottages, also painting door jambs and window frames with cement; fitting in and out blocks in European range, also fitting new plates at each side of oven in cook-house, and general repairs to the range in warders' cottages; fitting a new incandescent boiler in kitchen of Governor's quarters; repairing and painting Governor's office; repairing valve of gas main; repairing crank pump, and supplying new pipe for same; taking down and re-setting chimney shaft of Governor's quarters; taking down the defective gas supply pipe to B wing, and replacing same with 2-inch G. B. gas pipe; supplying and setting a copper circulating cylinder to range in Governor's quarters; repairing electric bells; taking down and re-setting a chimney shaft over Governor's office.
Do.,	Prison,	Removing drinking water tap from W.C.'s and fixing same on corridors; whitewashing and painting clerk's office; whitewashing cells and painting cell doors; painting water pipes and gas pipes; putting down two new lengths of sewer pipes; putting new rim lock on front gate; whitestanding and painting walls of hall leading to male prison; constructing yard attached to Governor's quarters; removing wall from under arch of A wing; fitting up new washstand stand and sanitary basin in Governor's quarters; making four new rock harrows; whitewashing walls and ceilings of male hall, yards of prison, and outer walls of hospital; repairing water and gas pipes, and roofs of prison; cleaning gutters and repairing down pipes; painting front gate, erecting new execution chamber, repairing locks, and replacing glass where broken through the prison; repairing cisterns and water taps in cottages and prison.

TABLE XXIII.—WORKS OF RECONSTRUCTION, REPAIRS, &c.—*continued.*

Prison.	Labour (Contract or Prison).	Detail of Works.
Spike Island .	Contract,	Papering and painting, &c., clerks' quarters; rough coating walls of Governor's house; repairing electric bells from prison to Governor's house and hospital.
Do.,	Prison, ,	Staining dining-room floor and staircase in Governor's house; repairing W.C. in Deputy-Governor's house, and both rooms in lieu of A wing; removing wall which accompanied hospital yard; breaking doorway from officers' mess to apportioned room in new store building, so as to convert this room into a dormitory for officers, and erecting a lavatory and W.C. in landing attached to same; ... dormitory; repairing and plastering the cells ... B wing; ... Protestant chapel, officers' mess, front entrance hall, bath ... passage, and general ... ... dry washing throughout the prison; repairing ... baths, down pipes from eave shoots of Governor's house and reception room; putting up six windows (Cathedral glass) in R.C. chapel; papering two sitting rooms and one bedroom in Deputy-Governor's house; erecting syphon cistern in A wing W.C.; repairing walls, gongs, gaslightings, &c., throughout the prison.
Limerick Male,	Contract,	Repairing weighbridge; repairing electric bells in Governor's and clerks' offices; repairing water-pipes leading to two of the W.C.'s in male prison; fitting up water tap on pipe in married exercise yard; fixing up two taps on pipes in main prison.
Do.,	Prison, ,	Fitting up new door and frame to gas house; painting slates of front gate lamps; fitting up new frame and eaves for well in wood-yard; repairing part of cook house floor with tiles; fitting up eave pipes on stone sheds; fitting up door on servitor of No. 4 block; laying new concrete path in married exercise yard; repairing several leak ... upon in gas pipes, water pipes, and heating pipes; scraping and painting gas pipes red; scraping and painting water pipes blue; taking off and replacing plastering of stairs in officers' quarters; executing general glazing and whitewashing.
Limerick Female,	Contract,	Repairing the several roofs of building; whitewashing all exterior walls, and painting with umber in all exposed ironwork of prison; breaking off, re-plastering, daubing, and colouring walls of front entrance and gate warders' quarters; rectifying stone and wooden stairs leading to places of worship; colouring interior of Protestant chapel, and varnishing all woodwork; whitening stairs, ceiling, and ... several rooms; ... walls of yards adjoining courthouse and chief warder's yard; sundry repairs to ... of laundry, and to gas, heating, and water pipes throughout prison.
Do.,	Prison,	Repairing gas and water pipes; whitewashing, painting, glazing, and minor repairs throughout prison.
Londonderry,	Contract,	Repairing and refitting water cocks, closets gas mains and brackets, water and gas pipes and heating stoves of prison; fixing a new ... in cook house, a new ironing stove in laundry, and heating stove in R.C. chapel; fixing with ... lead the hot water supply tank in female prison; papering and painting two rooms in Governor's house, two bedrooms in chief warder's quarters, ceiling of matron's room and Governor's office; fixing a food hoist in Governor's house, also a ...; repairing electric bells and keeping them in order, also the ... burners and gas lamps of prison.

TABLE XXIII.—WORKS of RECONSTRUCTION, REPAIRS, &c.—*continued.*

Prison.	Labour (Contract or Prison).	Details of Works.
Londonderry, .	Prison, .	Fitting up five new window frames for punishment cells, glazing and painting same; making a new door frame and fixing same in R.C. Chapel; fixing a new lever latch in surgery door; making carpentry work for [illegible] boxes of Governor's house; removing fire tiles, and performing the necessary repairs to ranges and firegrates in prisoners' cookhouse, officers' mess room, Governor's and chief warder's quarters; repairing bells in cells of male and female prisons, also doors, windows, and locks of same; removing old stone floor in one of the rooms in hospital, and fixing a wooden flooring in same; fixing two new locks in officers' quarters; performing general repairs to closets, eave gutters, and roofs of prison; flagging pathway in male prisoners' exercise yards, 240 feet in length and 2½ feet wide; lowering the walls in the exercise yards 5 feet, to the length of 310 feet, also the walls of debtors' yard lowered by 11 feet to the length of 140 feet; painting all doors, windows, staircases, and whitewashing all cells, halls, rooms, and inside walls of prison.
Sligo, . . .	Contract,	Laying down sewer pipe from weighbridge to existing sewer; erecting new heating cylinder in Governor's house; repairing cold water tank in laundry and water pipe in cookhouse yard; erecting new earthenware sink in gate quarters; repairing roof of Church; hot water pipe in laundry and bath room; renewing cast-iron casing to cookhouse boiler; repairing water pipe in wood yard.
Do., . . .	Prison, .	Taking down two walls at coal yard; erecting one and rebuilding corner of solitary cells; altering lumber room into a punishment cell; taking down eight feet of wall at female prison, and resetting stone; pointing gable of hospital; whitewashing, colouring, and painting church and chapel, and painting surgery; opening and clearing sewer at weighbridge; erecting railings in yard at back of cookhouse and [illegible]; making and erecting two doors in chief warder's quarters; papering two rooms in cottage at gate; rebuilding [illegible] and repairing door jambs; putting new window frame in Governor's office; general repairs, painting, limewashing, &c., throughout the prison.
Tralee, . . .	Contract,	Cleaning out two cesspits; general plumbing and repairs; repairing laundry boiler; supplying water for garden from back of officers' quarters; painting and repairing dome and roof of male prison, and roofs of female prison and stores; putting up down pipe at end of coal store; papering and painting Governor's house; repairing bells and locks; sheeting cistern with lead.
Do., . . .	Prison, .	Cleaning and coping 31 yards of boundary wall; limewashing kitchen and laundry of female prison; putting up [illegible] range in female prison; [illegible] of fire bars, fire bricks, and flue of sheet-iron from range to chimney; putting new bars on two windows in reception passage, and leading into stonework; scraping and painting [illegible] gas pipes of male prison; limewashing cells of male and female prisons; making new frame for flowers and early plants; repairing two new doors and frames and wooden front gate; limewashing boundary wall, wall of buildings, cells of male and female prisons; coating with gravel space in front of warders' cottages and entrance gates, and between entrance gates; painting administrative block doors; taking down and cleaning gas pipes of thirteen cells in female prison; laying down new flooring in chief warder's kitchen and altering stairs and doorway; painting doors, gates, and railings throughout prison.
Tullamore, . .	Contract,	Cleaning cesspool, &c., at delivery of main sewer; erecting new wash-out closet and trap in right wing of prison; repairing water pipes; erecting new two hundred dry gas meter; repairing gas pipes; putting up new electric bell for communicating from prison with Governor; erecting new three-ton cart weighbridge.

TABLE XXIII.—WORKS OF RECONSTRUCTION, REPAIRS, &c.—*continued.*

PRISONS.	Labour (Contract or Prison).	Detail of Works.
Tullamore, . .	Prison, .	Painting and whitewashing male and female prisons; laying down new waste water pipe from bath in right wing; putting up new length of eave gutter in female prison; making sundry small repairs and improvements; setting two type boxes, one in each wing; setting Stanley range in cottage; putting in two new cell window frames in right wing; taking down framework and iron railings in chapel; erecting shelving in female prison; making two new closet seats; glazing of prison, and painting roofs of male and female divisions.
Waterford, . .	Contract,	Supplying and erecting four heavy wooden gates for yards in prison; a new laundry stove in laundry, and the following in Governor's house:—a new range in kitchen, [illegible] sets of china furniture, and two brass [illegible]; two new pendants, and new chain on gaselier in dining room; also papering, whitening, and painting house; repairing water cock; a new high pressure ball cock in closet; five chimney pots, and repairs to windows, doors, grates, bells, locks, keys, and gas fittings; a night latch lock for hall door; supplying and erecting two soot doors in Governor's office chimney, seven washing troughs in laundry, one cooking stove in matron's quarters, one register grate in Governor's office, one sham register grate in clerk's office, two sham registers in guardroom, one in [illegible] cell, one in storeroom, one in male officers' quarters, one in matron's quarters, and three in hospitals; twelve galvanized locks for work sheds; one rim lock for photo house; two rim locks officers' quarters; a new saddle boiler for heating water for baths and cookhouse; a new range plate for range in cookhouse; repairing laundry stove door; painting and varnishing front entrance gate, and painting iron rails outside prison gate; repairing gas pipes, pendants, brackets, water pipes, cocks, down pipes, pumps, through part of prison, viz., front gate, offices, male hall, hospitals, stores, officers' quarters, Governor's house, laundry, furnace room, and yard.
Do., . .	Prison, .	Erecting a new communion rails in front of altar in chapel; whitening ceiling, and papering walls of Governor's office; papering [illegible] matrons' rooms; repairing seats of water closets; excavating a channel in front of stone sheds; relaying portion of spiral stairs, and part of corridors in male prison, also part of guardroom and male officers' rooms; plastering part of hospital, patches in hospital yard and laundry and stone yard; general whitewashing, painting, varnishing, glazing, &c., done throughout the prison, store rooms, officers' quarters (male and female), basement of Governor's house, guard-house, laundry, hospitals, and work shops.
Wexford, . .	Contract,	Erecting new range and gas fittings in the officers' mess.
Do., . .	Prison, .	Papering small sitting room and part of staircase in Governor's quarters; repairing wire railing in front of prison; putting a new sash and frame in the chief warder's quarters, and covering a shed in chief warder's yard; erecting new gas lamp over entrance gate; making a new door at entrance to Governor's garden; repairing eaveboards; re-coping and pointing with cement gate-keeper's quarters and boundary wall; raising flue of matron's quarters with zinc; recovering roof of photograph house with asphalt; enamelling baths in bath house; painting, whitewashing, plastering, and erecting shelves in officers' mess; general repairs to building, including carpentry, plumbing, plastering, painting, glazing, and whitewashing.

TABLE XXIII.—WORKS OF RECONSTRUCTION, REPAIRS, &c.—*continued.*

MINOR PRISONS.

Minor Prisons.	Labour (Contract or Prison).	Detail of Works.
Carrick-on-Shannon,	Contract,	Supplying and setting range in chief warder's quarters; boarding two rooms in chief warder's quarters; cleaning all chimneys in prison; pointing with cement the chimney stacks and ridge tiles of main prison, the Governor's house and lodge.
Do.,	Prison,	Painting entrance doors of prison lodge, Governor's house and windows; general whitewashing and painting corridors, stairs, &c., in main prison.
Dungannon,	Contract,	Carrying out sundry repairs to roofs and water pipes, and chief warder's quarters.
Do.,	Prison,	Carrying out general repairs and minor works of maintenance.
Enniskillen,	Contract,	Lifting and resetting stone steps at entrance gate; puttying and painting glass dome; rebuilding new chimney on laundry; renewing ridge tiles thereon, and new eave gutters; putting in new down pipes from eave gutters, old female prison; cleaning eave gutters through the entire buildings, and repairing broken slates; repairing heating apparatus.
Do.,	Prison,	Whitewashing and glazing throughout the prison.
Lifford,	Contract,	Fixing new stove pipe to range in kitchen; repairing and painting four rooms and hall of chief warder's quarters; removing old pan, W.C., and putting in new wash down W.C. with syphon cistern; repairing pump to W.C. in above quarters; repairing chimney shaft; repairing pump to office, W.C.; repairing land gutter; whitewashing and painting office and porch.
Do.,	Prison,	Repairing floor in laundry; whitewashing window sashes and putting on new sash fasteners in chief warder's quarters and office; repairing and putting pump in working order in laundry; fixing new bars to two cell windows; fitting wire netting to railing on platform around chief warder's quarters; making and fitting up a common new window blinds in chief warder's quarters; carrying out general repairs and minor works of maintenance.
Omagh,	Contract,	Repairing stove in warder's quarters; supplying and fixing up new closet and cistern in chief warder's quarters; laying a lead pipe with drinking water from male prison to female prison; repairing two broken flags in veranda round Governor's house; general repairs to large weighbridge.
Do.,	Prison,	Repairing front of heating furnace; glazing windows, repairing bells; carrying out whitewashing, painting, plastering, and roof work, as required; setting in gas burners where necessary; repairing gas and water taps; controlling two baths; repairing fleshings and skirtings with cement; repairing two wooden doors, and putting up twenty-four feet of main water pipe at front gate.
Wicklow,	Contract,	Plastering portion of office walls; cleaning nine sheets round prison; fixing new cap on ventilator; repairing lead gutter on Governor's house; repairing pump in No. 1 yard; taking down and removing two small walls in exercise yards; repairing gas in Governor's house.
Do.,	Prison,	Carrying out general repairs and minor works of maintenance, viz., whitewashing cells, halls, closets, and yards; painting gates, doors, and cells throughout the prison.

TABLE XXIII.—WORKS OF RECONSTRUCTION, REPAIRS, &c.—*continued.*

BRIDEWELLS.

Bridewells.	Labour (Contract or Prison.)	Details of Work.
Ballieboro', . .	Contract.	Repairing roof of bridewell; clearing sewers between W.C.'s and main drain; carrying out sundry general repairs.
Bantry, . .	Contract,	Repairing sewer pipes, eave sheets, and walks in exercise yards.
Do , .	Prison, .	General repairs to painting and whitewashing.
Cahirciveen, . .	Contract,	Tarring of coal-shed and ____.
Clifden, . .	Contract,	Nil.
Do., . .	Prison, .	Carrying out necessary limewashing and painting by keeper in bridewell.
Kilrush, . .	Contract,	Cleaning ___-pits in male and female prisons; cleaning four chimneys; whitewashing front and end walls of bridewell.
Loughrea, . .	Contract,	Carrying out necessary chimney cleaning in bridewell.
Do., . .	Prison, .	Carrying out necessary limewashing in bridewell.
Mallow, . .	Prison, .	Papering two rooms in keeper's quarters and general repairs to painting and whitewashing
Newry, . .	Contract,	Carrying out sundry general repairs.
Parsonstown, .	Contract,	Re-plastering walls, painting windows, doors, bars, and railings.
Do. . .	Prison, .	Painting doors, woodwork, &c., of bridewell.
Youghal, . .	Contract,	Repairing cooking range.
Do., . .	Prison, .	General repairs to painting and whitewashing.

TABLE XXIII.—WORKS OF RECONSTRUCTION, REPAIRS, &c.—continued.

CONVICT PRISON.

CONVICT PRISON.	Labour (Contract or Prison.)	Detail of Work.
Maryborough, Do.,	Contract. Prison.	Repairing electric bells; fixing hot boiler in kitchen; repairing pump in deep well. Continuing the building of the concrete wall enclosing the prison farm to the length of 600 yards; building yard walls of piggery and concreting floor of yards; excavating and filling with concrete the foundation for enlargement of prison 340 yards long; quarrying stone on farm, thereby obtaining a supply for the various works in progress; putting six new fireplaces in offices and officers' quarters; fixing and re-setting boilers in kitchen and piggery; whitewashing and painting the interior of each division of the prison and officers' quarters; repairing electric bells; hanging fifteen window blinds in Medical Officer's quarters; repairing roofs of prison and carrying out general repairs and minor works of maintenance.

LOCAL AND CONVICT PRISON.

	Contract. Prison.	
Mountjoy, Do.,	Contract. Prison.	Supplying and sinking two new steam boilers, 18 feet long, adjoining laundry of female prison, for heating the drying closet, supplying hot water to wash-tubs, baths, &c., and supplying steam to kitchen for cooking purposes; supplying and fixing up ironwork rails in drying closet, including steam coils, cast-iron doors, galvanized heaters, rails, &c.; supplying and putting in position two large cast-iron tanks for connecting with steam boilers to supply hot and cold water to laundry, baths, &c., and to provide a supply of water to steam boilers when required; fixing up machinery for new fumigating house in female prison. Altering laundry in female prison, including the removal of lower part of end wall of laundry to make space for steam boilers, and building additional space for sinking, &c., forming culverts and flues from boilers to large chimney stack; forming a drying closet with front wall, steel joists, concrete arching, &c.; preparing and fixing twenty new washtubs in laundry, including divisions, channels, &c., for drainage, and fitting with hot and cold water supply from cisterns over boilers; connecting baths with hot water cisterns over boilers; fitting up a large room east of laundry for store; building new fitting house on grounds east of D wing; forming new reception at south side of A division male prison, excavating and removing 560 cubic yards of surface, building concrete walls and fixing roof timbers, underpinning old walls and putting down 45 yards of new sewerage, including three inspection chambers; forming new coal stores at north side of B and C division male prison, excavating and removing 850 cubic yards of surface, building concrete walls, underpinning old walls, putting down 20 yards of new sewer, and forming roof with steel joists and concrete arches; altering basement B division male prison to form reception cells, including internal walls, floors, windows, doors, heating pipes, gas and water supply, and auxiliary arrangements; altering three separation exercise yards to connect with local wing of male prison; fixing up workshops for plumbers, locksmiths, and brushmakers; fitting up temporary visiting room adjoining A division male prison; repairing boilers, ranges, &c., and setting new heat boiler in kitchen of hospital, female prison, and new saddle boiler for heating cells in female prison; repairing roofs and roof lights, including old and new roof lights in corridors of hospital of female prison; making new van and new cart for Mountjoy Male Prison; making sixteen new cell doors for Castlebar Prison, two farm carts made for Maryborough Prison, also wheel barrows; spade for Tullamore, Kilmainham, Waterford, and Clonmel Prisons; cleaning, papering, and painting boardrooms of female prison, and cleaning and painting corridor; cleaning, papering, and painting four rooms in Governor's house; cleaning, papering, and painting Deputy Governor's house; cleaning, colouring, and painting six warders' cottages; cleaning and lime-washing cells, corridors, &c., of prison and hospitals, and painting woodwork and ironwork; cleaning and painting entrance gates and railings; cleaning and repairing roads, paths, boundaries, &c.

TABLE XXIV.—RETURNS SHOWING EMPLOYMENT OF PRISONERS IN LOCAL AND CONVICT PRISONS AND ESTIMATED VALUE OF THEIR EARNINGS.

(As required by 40-41 Vict., cap. 49, section 16).

(*A.*) *Return showing the Prisons in which each Description of Employment has been carried on during the Year.*

Description of Employment.	Prisons in which carried on.	Total Number of ...
I.—In Manufactures:—		
Baking	Cork M., Mountjoy M. Convict	2
Brushmaking	Mountjoy Local.	1
Knitting and needleworking.	Armagh, Belfast, Castlebar, Cork F., Limerick F., Londonderry, Mountjoy F. Local, Sligo, Tullamore, Waterford, Drogheda, Mountjoy F. Convict.	19
Making Mail bags . . .	Kilmainham, Mountjoy M. Local, and Mountjoy M. convict.	3
Matmaking, plaiting, and other work connected therewith.	Belfast, Clonmel, Cork M., Dundalk, Galway, Kilkenny, Limerick M., Londonderry, Mountjoy Local, Sligo, Wexford, Mountjoy M. Convict.	10
Picking or teasing oakum, hair, &c.	All prisons except Cork F., Limerick F., Maryborough, Mountjoy F. Local, and Mountjoy F. Convict.	24
Sackmaking and bagmaking	Armagh, Dundalk, Kilmainham, Londonderry, Mountjoy Local, Tullamore.	6
Shoemaking	Belfast, Cork M., Kilkenny, Limerick M., Mountjoy M. Local, Tralee, Tullamore, Maryborough, Mountjoy M. Convict.	9
Smithing	Belfast, Cork M., Kilkenny, Kilmainham, Londonderry, Tullamore, Waterford.	7
Stonebreaking . . .	Armagh, Belfast, Castlebar, Clonmel, Cork M., Galway, Kilkenny, Kilmainham, Limerick M., Londonderry, Sligo, Tralee, Waterford, Wexford, Drogheda, Randalstown, Mullingar, Omagh.	18
Tailoring	Belfast, Tullamore, Waterford, Maryborough, Mountjoy M Convict.	5
Washing, not including prisoners' clothing.	Armagh, Belfast, Castlebar, Clonmel, Cork F., Galway, Limerick F., Londonderry, Mountjoy F. Local, Sligo, Tralee, Tullamore, Wexford.	13
Woodcutting . . .	Armagh, Belfast, Clonmel, Cork M., Dundalk, Galway, Kilkenny, Kilmainham, Limerick M., Londonderry, Mountjoy M. Local, Sligo, Tralee, Tullamore, Waterford, Wexford, Drogheda, Rathkillen.	16
Linen cutting . . .	Belfast	1
Weaving	Mountjoy Local.	1
Tinsmithing . . .	Clonmel, Sligo, Mountjoy M. Convict.	3
Carpentry . . .	Cork M., Mountjoy M. Convict, Tralee .	3
Agriculture . . .	Belfast, Tralee, Maryborough, . . .	3

(*A.*)—*continued*—*Return showing the Prisons in which each Description of Employment has been carried on during the Year.*

Description of Employment.	Prisons in which carried on.	Total Number of Prisons.
I.—In Buildings:—		
Bricklayers or masons,	Belfast, Clonmel, Cork M., Londonderry, Mountjoy M. Local, Tralee, Waterford, Mullingar.	8
Carpenters or joiners,	Armagh, Belfast, Castlebar, Clonmel, Cork M., Dundalk, Galway, Kilmainham, Limerick M., Londonderry, Mountjoy M. Local, Sligo, Tralee, Tullamore, Wexford, Omagh, Maryborough, Mountjoy M. Convict.	18
Labourers,	All prisons except Castlebar, Clonmel, Cork F., Limerick F., Maryboro' F. Local, Sligo, Wexford, Carrick, Drogheda, Enniskillen, Wicklow, and Mountjoy F. Convict.	18
Painters and glaziers,	All prisons except Cork F., Mountjoy F. Local, Maryborough, and Mountjoy F. Convict.	25
Plasterers,	Belfast, Kilkenny, Kilmainham, Sligo, Enniskillen, Omagh.	6
Plumbers and gasfitters,	Belfast, Kilkenny, Kilmainham,	3
Smiths,	Belfast, Cork M., Dundalk, Galway, Tralee, Wexford, Omagh, Maryborough, Mountjoy M. Convict.	9
Whitewashers,	All prisons except Maryborough, and Mountjoy F. Convict.	27
Stonebreaking for concreting, &c.	Mountjoy Local,	1
III.—In the ordinary service of the Prison :—		
Carpentry,	Cork M.,	1
Cleaning and jobbing work in and about the prison, &c.	All prisons,	29
Cooking for the prisoners,	All prisons except Mountjoy F. Local, Carrick Enniskillen, Mullingar, Omagh, Wicklow.	23
Labourers,	Kilmainham,	1
Nursing and attending sick prisoners, children, &c.	Armagh, Belfast, Clonmel, Cork M., Dundalk, Galway, Tullamore, Kilmainham, Limerick M., Limerick F., Kilkenny, Londonderry, Mountjoy M. Local, Sligo, Tralee, Waterford, Drogheda, Enniskillen, Mullingar, Omagh, Mountjoy M. Convict.	21
Pumping water for the prison,	Castlebar, Clonmel, Cork M., Dundalk, Kilkenny, Limerick M, Waterford, Wexford, Carrick-on-Shannon, Mullingar, Wicklow.	11
Repairing all kinds of prison clothing and bedding	All prisons except Mountjoy Convict and Mountjoy F. Convict	27
Repairing all kinds of prison shoes.	Armagh, Belfast, Castlebar, Clonmel, Cork M., Dundalk, Galway, Kilkenny, Kilmainham, Limerick M., Londonderry, Mountjoy M. Local, Sligo, Tralee, Tullamore and Wexford.	16
Repairing all kinds of prison utensils.	Armagh, Belfast, Clonmel, Cork M., Kilkenny.	5
Repairing and binding books, &c.	Cork M., Londonderry, Mountjoy M. Convict,	3
Stoking prison furnaces,	Belfast, Kilkenny, Kilmainham, Limerick M., Londonderry, Tullamore, Waterford, Mountjoy M. Convict.	8
Washing prisoners' clothing,	All prisons except Limerick M. and Mountjoy F. Convict.	27
Woodcutting,	Kilmainham, Mullingar, Wicklow.	3
Gardening,	Clonmel, Cork F., Dundalk, Galway, Kilkenny, Londonderry, Sligo, Enniskillen, Mullingar.	9

(B.)—*Separate Returns from each Prison.*

ARMAGH PRISON.

Return by the Governor, showing the employment of the Prisoners and value of their Earnings during the year ended 31st March, 1872.

Description of Employment.	Daily Average Number of Prisoners (for working days of the year).			Value of Prisoners' Labour.	Total.
	M.	F.	Total	£ s. d.	£ s. d.
In Manufactures:—					
Knitting and needlework, &c.,	—	5·46	5·46	0 7 8	
Picking or teazing oakum, hair, &c.,	17·84	1·86	19·74	21 9 7	
Bookmaking,	16·85	·18	16·73	24 15 7	
Shoemaking,	11·76	—	11·76	64 17 12	
Washing, and making prisoners' clothing,	—	1·	1·	0 15 11	
Woodmaking,	6·24	—	6·24	87 6 1	
Total,	46·75	8·19	56·96		149 13 4
In Buildings:—					
Carpenters or joiners,	·78	—	·78	1 17 6	
Labourers,	·19	—	·19	4 15 0	
Painters and glaziers,	·48	—	·48	19 19 0	
Whitewashers,	·49	—	·49	19 4 6	
Total,	1·94	—	1·94		39 15 2
In the ordinary service of the Prison:—					
Cleaning and jobbing work in and about the prison and prison yard and buildings (exclusive of building work of any kind),	4·14	·51	6·46	49 14 0	
Cooking for the prisoners,	3·63	—	3·36	104 7 2	
Nursing and attending sick prisoners,	·03	·31	·34	18 7 6	
Repairing all kinds of prison clothing,	·16	4·03	1·13	12 6 0	
Repairing all kinds of prison shoes,	·81	—	·81	5 10 3	
Repairing all kinds of prison utensils,	·12	—	·12	7 5 0	
Washing prisoners' clothing,	—	5·34	5·96	63 16 0	
Total,	7·24	9·44	14·76		257 19 0
Non-effective:—					
Sick,	1·41	·44	7·15	—	
Under punishment,	·48	11	·40	—	
Unemployed:—					
Awaiting trial,	1·4	5·	7·4	—	
Debtors,	·07	—	·06	—	
First class misdemeanants,	1·	·43	1·77	—	
Others, &c.,	1·14	·41	1·37	—	
Total,	5·48	5·93	7·93	—	
Grand Total,	59·93	16·45	89·	—	540 0 9

BELFAST PRISON.

Return by the Governor, showing the employment of the Prisoners and value of their Earnings during the year ended 31st March, 1899.

Description of Employment.	Daily Average Number of Prisoners (for working days of the year).			Value of Prisoners' Labour.			Total.		
	M.	F.	Total	£	s.	d.	£	s.	d.
In Manufactures :—									
Knitting and needleworking	—	34 27	34 27	483	3	8			
Matmaking, plaiting, and other work con-									
nected therewith	11 54	—	54 54	137	14	3			
Picking (including oakum, hair, &c.)	33 43	—	33 43	69	16	3			
Shoemaking	11 74	—	11 74	811	15	8			
Smithing	34	—	34	13	17	6			
Stonebreaking	77 18	—	99 18	345	11	8			
Tailoring	7 43	—	7 53	191	1	6			
Washing, incl. prisoners' clothing	104	11 87	11 37	84	10	10			
Woodcutting	6 39	—	6 39	10	17	0			
Agriculture	1000	—	1000	118	15	0			
Lime cutting	—	3001	3001	147	18	3			
Total	93109	1597	368 06				1,594	14	8
In Buildings :—									
Bricklayers or masons	7 34	—	7 34	84	19	2			
Carpenters or joiners	1 34	—	1 34	40	1	8			
Labourers	3979	—	37 79	433	16	8			
Painters and glaziers	7 93	—	7 93	64	1	7			
Plumbers and gasfitters	30	—	30	13	10	9			
Smiths	1 03	—	1 03	34	17	8			
Window cleaners	87	36	1 23	13	11	7			
Total	53 74	36	4616				871	3	1
In the ordinary service of the Prison :—									
Cleaning and jobbing work in and about the prison and prison yard, and buildings (exclusive of building work of any kind)	18 52	3 91	31 43	443	18	10			
Cooking for the prisoners	4 41	—	4 41	167	4	10			
Nursing and attending sick prisoners	43	—	64	11	5	7			
Repairing all kinds of prison clothing	4 83	6 17	10 60	100	17	8			
Repairing all kinds of prison shoes	9 11	—	7 51	61	4	3			
Repairing all kinds of prison utensils	24	—	73	4	14	0			
Stoking prison furnaces	30	—	30	17	11	0			
Washing prisoners' clothing	—	4 48	4 48	84	10	10			
Total	33 41	14 54	4871				1,013	11	8

CASTLEBAR PRISON.

Return by the Governor, showing the employment of the Prisoners and value of their Earnings during the year ended 31st March, 1899.

Description of Employment.	Daily Average Number of Prisoners (for working days of the year).			Value of Prisoners' Labour.	Total.
	M.	F.	Total.	£ s. d.	£ s. d.
In Manufactures:—					
Knitting and needleworking,	—	3·25	3·25		
Picking or teasing oakum, &c.,	1·90	—	1·90	0 15 10	
Stonebreaking,	13·15	—	13·15	10 9 9	
Washing, not including prisoners' clothing,	—	·70	·70	2 7 10	
Total,	14·05	3·9	17·95		41 9 9
In Buildings:—					
Carpenters or Joiners,	·63	—	·63	1 7 9	
Painters and Glaziers,	·15	—	·15	4 5 4	
Whitewashers,	·20	—	·20	7 11 4	
Total,	·98	—	·98		13 18 1
In the ordinary service of the Prison:—					
Cleaning and keeping work in and about the prison and prison yard and buildings (exclusive of building work of any kind),	4·65	1·9	5·93	119 13 6	
Cooking for the prisoners,	1·	—	1·	44 10 7	
Pumping water for the service of the prison only,	·70	—	·70	4 14 4	
Repairing all kinds of prison clothing,	·36	1·26	1·70	42 3 10	
Repairing all kinds of prison shoes,	·15	—	·15	2 10 10	
Washing prisoners' clothing,	—	1·75	1·75	13 2 10	
Total,	6·29	4·41	10·73		226 11 6
Non-effective:—					
Sick,	·30	·72	·72	—	
Under punishment,	·74	·46	·21	—	
Unemployed:—					
Awaiting trial,	1·40	·14	1·54	—	
First class misdemeanants,	·24	·46	·71	—	
Others, &c.,	8·94	1·19	5·34	—	
Total,	4·21	1·74	6·97	—	
Grand Total,	25·45	9·98	35·33	—	298 19 5

CLONMEL (MALE) PRISON.

Return by the Governor, showing the employment of the Prisoners and value of their Earnings during the year ended 31st March, 1899.

Description of Employment.	Daily Average Number of Prisoners (for working days of the year).	Value of Prisoners' Labour.	Total.
	n.	£ s. d.	£ s. d.
In Manufactures:—			
Matmaking, plaiting, and other work connected therewith, .	4·7f	13 16 4	
Picking or teasing oakum, hair, &c. . .	12·14	3 4 1	
Shoemaking, ...	3·4f	11 5 0	
Tin smithing, ...	·16	4 16 0	
Weaving, not including prisoners' clothing, .	8·79	103 0 4	
Woodturning, ...	2·34	13 17 7	
Total, ...	77·16		163 7 5
In Buildings:—			
Bricklayers or masons, ...	·24	10 14 0	
Carpenters or joiners, ...	·23	15 0 0	
Painters and glaziers, ...	·31	1 4 4	
Whitewashers, ...	·23	6 14 0	
Total, ...	1·73		03 17 0
In the ordinary service of the Prison:—			
Cleaning and jobbing work in and about the prison and prison yard and buildings (exclusive of building work of any kind), .	18·91	343 4 2	
Cooking for the prisoners, ...	3·01	43 5 4	
Nursing and attending sick prisoners, . .	·94	1 16 0	
Pumping water for the service of the prison only,	2·24	49 11 0	
Repairing all kinds of prison clothing, .	·97	11 17 0	
Repairing all kinds of prison shoes, .	·40	16 16 1	
Repairing all kinds of prison utensils, .	·1	1 0 0	
Washing prisoners' clothing, . . .	3·	45 16 1	
Repairing building, ...	·4f	1 8 1	
Gardening, ...	·44	11 0 0	
Total, ...	39·04		449 9 10
Non-effective:—			
Sick, ...	2·7	—	
Under punishment, ...	·44	—	
Unemployed:—			
Awaiting trial, ...	1·91	—	
First class misdemeanants, . . .	·13	3 99	
Others, &c.	3·99	—	
Total, ...	17·71	—	
Grand Total, ...	77·04	—	766 19 6

I

CORK (MALE) PRISON.

Return by the Governor, showing the employment of the Prisoners and value of their Earnings during the year ended 31st March, 1899.

Description of Employment.	Daily Average Number of Prisoners (for working days of the year).	Value of Prisoners' Labour.	Total.
	n.	£ s. d.	£ s. d.
In Manufactures :—			
Matmaking, plaiting, and other work connected therewith,	52·19	16 7 10	
Picking or tearing oakum, hair, &c.,	44·46	14 1 10	
Shoemaking,	1·	19 10 0	
Smithing,	·07	0 16 0	
Stonebreaking,	36·50	20 10 0	
Woodcutting,	14·21	40 5 4	
Carpentry,	·14	22 10 0	
Baking,	1·79	37 17 0	
Total,	152·69		159 19 4
In Buildings :—			
Bricklayers or masons,	·90	2 16 0	
Carpenters or joiners,	1·	30 0 0	
Labourers,	1·89	37 2 0	
Painters and glaziers,	1·99	44 17 0	
Whitewashers,	1·49	30 17 4	
Total,	6·90		145 16 4
In the ordinary service of the Prison :—			
Cleaning and jobbing work in and about the prison and prison yard and buildings (exclusive of building work of any kind),	71·05	104 0 8	
Cooking for the prisoners,	8·	44 1 0	
Nursing and attending sick prisoners,	·94	8 0 0	
Pumping water for the service of the prison only,	3·90	16 15 0	
Repairing all kinds of prison clothing,	9·54	164 7 0	
Repairing all kinds of prison shoes,	8·47	61 16 2	
Repairing all kinds of prison utensils,	·90	3 12 0	
Washing prisoners' clothing,	9·04	44 5 0	
Repairing books,	·47	6 18 7	
Carpentry,	·27	9 4 0	
Total,	44·27		454 12 5
Non-effective :—			
Sick,	8·24	—	
Under punishment,	1·78	—	
Unemployed :—			
Awaiting trial,	1·48	—	
Debtors,	·10	—	
First class misdemeanants,	1·86	—	
Others, &c.,	72·94	—	
Total,	55·91	—	
Grand Total,	80·76	—	1,322 7 6

CORK (FEMALE) PRISON.

Return by the Chief Warder, showing the employment of the Prisoners and value of their Earnings during the year ended 31st March, 1899.

Description of Employment.	Daily Average Number of Prisoners (for working days of the year).	Value of Prisoners' Labour.	Total.
	F.	£ s. d.	£ s. d.
In Manufactures:—			
Knitting and needleworking,	46·25	137 17 8	
Washing, not including prisoners' clothing,	1·	6 5 F	144 0 10
Total,	47·25		
In Buildings:—			
Whitewashing,	·40	10 7 5	10 1 0
In the ordinary service of the Prison:—			
Cleaning and jobbing work in and about the prison and prison yard and buildings (exclusive of building work of any kind),	7·55	140 12 4	
Cooking for the prisoners,	1·	25 12 10	
Repairing all kinds of prison clothing,	5·	37 15 6	
Washing prisoners' clothing,	5·90	54 11 5	
Gardening,	·75	15 17 1	275 15 0
Total,	16·05		
Non-effective:—			
Sick,	5·	—	
Under punishment,	0·26	—	
Unemployed:—			
Awaiting trial,	7·48	—	
First class misdemeanants,	·30	—	
Others, &c.,	13·77	—	
Total,	19·77	—	
Grand Total,	86·65	—	1,018 1 3

DUNDALK (MALE) PRISON.

Return by the Governor, showing the employment of the Prisoners and value of their Earnings during the year ended 31st March, 1899.

Description of Employment.	Daily Average Number of Prisoners (for working days of the year).	Value of Prisoners' Labour.	Total.
	M.	£ s. d.	£ s. d.
In Manufactures:—			
Rag-making,	4·65	13 10 4	
Mat-making, plaiting, and other work connected therewith,	19·06	46 10 0	
Picking or teasing cocoa-nut, hair, &c.,	15·86	16 10 5	
Woodcutting,	2·55	17 10 5	84 11 0
Total,	42·07		

I 2

DUNDALK (MALE) PRISON—*continued.*

Return by the Governor, showing the employment of the Prisoners and value of their Earnings during the year ended 31st March, 1899.

Description of Employment.	Daily Average Number of Prisoners (for working days of the year).	Value of Prisoners' Labour.	Total.
	N.	£ s. d.	£ s. d.
In Buildings :—			
Carpenters or Joiners,	73	4 19 1	
Labourers,	17	116 3 0	
Painters and glaziers,	44	18 18 4	
Smiths,	45	1 19 3	
Whitewashers,	7	18 6 1	
Total,	1·91		149 15 9
In the ordinary service of the Prison :—			
Cleaning and jobbing work in and about the prison and prison yard and buildings (exclusive of building work of any kind),	9·20	119 18 5	
Cooking for the prisoners,	7·	59 19 1	
Nursing and attending sick prisoners,	·46	1 7 3	
Pumping water for the service of the prison only,	9·79	77 16 6	
Repairing all kinds of prison clothing,	7·91	55 9 7	
Repairing all kinds of prison shoes,	1·71	71 11 5	
Washing prisoners' clothing,	1·70	90 14 5	
Gardening,	4 1	69 16 7	
Total,	99·		459 1 9
Non-effective :—			
Sick,	·74	—	
Under punishment,	·43	—	
Unemployed :—			
Awaiting trial,	7 07	—	
Debtors,	·07	—	
First class misdemeanants,	·74	—	
Others, &c.,	6·44	—	
Total,	16 97	—	
Grand Total,	97 45	—	674 9 9

GALWAY PRISON.

Return by the Governor, showing the employment of the Prisoners and value of their Earnings during the year ended 31st March, 1899.

Description of Employment.	Daily Average Number of Prisoners (for working days of the year).			Value of Prisoners' Labour.	Total
	M.	F.	Total.	£ s. d.	£ s. d.
In Manufactures :—					
Matmaking, plaiting, and other work connected therewith,	10·45	—	10·45	10 14 0	
Picking or teasing oakum, hair, &c.,	7·6	—	7·6	2 6 6	
Stonebreaking,	76 76	—	76 76	43 10 7	
Washing, not including prisoners' clothing,	—	1·	1·	3 0 8	
Wood cutting,	6·17	—	6·17	95 0 0	
Total,	51 17	1·	66 77		59 13 11

GALWAY PRISON—*continued.*

RETURN by the GOVERNOR, showing the employment of the Prisoners and value of their Earnings during the year ended 31st March, 1899.

Description of Employment.	Daily Average Number of Prisoners (for working days of the year).			Value of Prisoners' Labour.			Total.		
	M.	F.	Total.	£	s.	d.	£	s.	d.
In Buildings :—									
Carpenters or joiners,	·07	—	·07	2	10	0			
Painters and glaziers,	·31	—	·31	16	11	10			
Smiths,	·13	—	·13	4	10	11			
Whitewashers,	·39	—	·39	7	4	5			
Total,	·79	—	·79				31	8	2
In the ordinary service of the Prison :—									
Cleaning and jobbing work in and about the prison and prison yard and buildings (exclusive of building work of any kind),	8·76	·34	9·11	172	10	5			
Cooking for the prisoners,	2·	—	2·	45	1	0			
Nursing and attending sick prisoners,	·13	1·66	1·79	40	18	7			
Repairing all kinds of prison clothing,	·34	5·99	9·79	165	5	0			
Repairing all kinds of prison shoes,	·48	—	·48	9	4	1			
Washing prisoners' clothing,	—	7·16	7·16	11	4	5			
Gardening,	1·33	—	1·33	72	19	6			
Total,	13·24	11·43	24·63				534	9	9
Non-effective :—									
Sick,	1·31	·72	1·43	—					
Under punishment,	·13	·02	·14	—					
Unemployed :—									
Awaiting trial,	8·04	·17	7·17	—					
First class misdemeanants,	·19	—	·12	—					
Others, &c.,	4·03	·72	4·46	—					
Total,	9·34	1·60	10·93	—					
Grand Total,	71·24	15·73	87·27	—			645	0	7

KILKENNY PRISON.

RETURN by the GOVERNOR, showing the employment of the Prisoners and value of their Earnings during the year ended 31st March, 1899.

Description of Employment.	Daily Average Number of Prisoners (for working days of the year).	Value of Prisoners' Labour.			Total.		
	M.	£	s.	d.	£	s.	d.
In Manufactures :—							
Matmaking, plaiting, and other work connected therewith,	7·1	8	16	5			
Picking or teasing oakum, hair, &c.,	14·48	16	1	11			
Shoemaking,	6·24	165	8	8			
Stonebreaking,	9·48	8	17	10			
Woodcutting,	1·96	23	12	9			
Total,	64·2				797	11	5
In Buildings :—							
Labourers,	·48	12	7	0			
Painters and glaziers,	·31	10	3	1			
Plasterers,	·01	8	7	5			
Whitewashers,	·63	10	9	1			
Total,	1·33				62	11	6

KILKENNY PRISON—*continued.*

Return by the Governor, showing the employment of the Prisoners and value of their Earnings during the year ended 31st March, 1899.

Description of Employment.	Daily Average Number of Prisoners (for working days of the year).	Value of Prisoners' Labour.	Total.
In the ordinary service of the Prison:—	n.	£ s. d	£ s. d.
Cleaning and jobbing work in and about the prison and prison yard and buildings (exclusive of building work of any kind),	11·65	014 16 5	
Cooking for the prisoners,	·73	41 13 7	
Nursing and attending sick prisoners,	·87	73 0 10	
Pumping water for the service of the prison only,	7·95	170 6 10	
Repairing all kinds of prison clothing,	4·84	97 0 8	
Repairing all kinds of prison shoes,	7·	49 14 5	
Repairing all kinds of prison utensils,	·5	4 10 10	
Stoking prison furnaces,	·66	16 17 31	
Washing prisoners' clothing,	3·78	45 6 3	
Gardening,	·77	16 15 1	
Total,	56·15		658 16 1
Non-effective:—			
Sick,	·73	—	
Under punishment,	·43	—	
Unemployed:—			
Awaiting trial,	5·93	—	
Debtors,	·73	—	
Others, &c.	9·68	—	
Total,	17·1	—	
Grand Total,	113·08	—	658 16 1

KILMAINHAM (MALE) PRISON.

Return by the Governor, showing the employment of the Prisoners and value of their Earnings during the year ended 31st March, 1899.

Description of Employment.	Daily Average Number of Prisoners (for working days of the year).	Value of Prisoners' Labour.	Total.
In Manufactures:—	n.	£ s. d.	£ s. d.
Picking or teasing oakum, hair, &c.,	84·91	16 10 7	
Sackmaking,	5·75	10 9 5	
Smithing,	·7	2 16 5	
Stonebreaking,	31·45	46 15 7	
Woodcutting,	11·85	34 11 11	
Making mail bags,	·65	3 6 5	
Total,	79·76		102 5 1
In Buildings:—			
Carpenters or Joiners,	·7	46 5 8	
Labourers,	7·	46 19 9	
Painters and glaziers,	·45	11 15 4	
Plasterers,	·7	7 13 4	
Plumbers and Gasfitters,	·8	4 11 4	
Whitewashers,	·83	20 19 1	
Total,	5·58		141 13 4

KILMAINHAM (MALE) PRISON—*continued.*

Return by the Governor, showing the employment of the Prisoners and value of their Earnings during the year ended 31st March, 1899.

Description of Employment.	Daily Average Number of Prisoners (for working days of the year).	Value of Prisoners' Labour.	Total.
	n.	£ s. d.	£ s. d.
In the ordinary service of the Prison:—			
Cleaning and jobbing work in and about the prison and prison yards and buildings (exclusive of building work of any kind),	10·66	120 17 9	
Cooking for the prisoners,	3·	101 15 9	
Nursing and attending sick prisoners,	·77	6 0 1	
Repairing all kinds of prison clothing,	76	19 4 9	
Repairing all kinds of prison shoes,	·6	16 1 0	
Clothing prison farmers,	2·	40 10 1	
Washing prisoners' clothing,	6·	34 11 9	
Woodsawing,	2·	16 3 6	
Labourers,	7·16	191 1 10	
Total,	21·66		167 17 1
Non-effective:—			
Sick,	5·8	—	
Under punishment,	·6	—	
Unemployed:—			
Awaiting trial,	13·71	—	
Debtors,	·73	—	
First class misdemeanants,	2·76	—	
Others, &c.,	17·21	—	
Total,	33·41	—	
Grand Total,	143·93	—	1,072 15 10

LIMERICK (MALE) PRISON.

Return by the Governor, showing the employment of the Prisoners and value of their Earnings during the year ended 31st March, 1899.

Description of Employment.	Daily Average Number of Prisoners (for working days of the year.)	Value of Prisoners' Labour.	Total.
	n.	£ s. d.	£ s. d.
In Manufacture:—			
Matmaking, picking, and other work connected therewith,	4·74	7 0 5	
Fishing or teasing calves, hair, &c.,	1·64	5 0 4	
Stonebreaking,	26·50	49 14 7	
Woodsawing,	11·24	64 0 9	
Total,	44·11		176 14 5

LIMERICK (MALE) PRISON—*continued.*

Return by the Governor, showing the employment of the Prisoners and value of their Earnings during the year ended 31st March, 1899.

Description of Employment.	Daily Average Number of Prisoners (for working days of the year).	Value of Prisoners' Labour.	Total.
	M.	£ s. d.	£ s. d.
In Buildings—			
Carpenters or joiners, ...	·21	7 0 10	
Labourers, ...	6 54	56 1 0	
Painters and glaziers, ...	·21	6 1 0	
Whitewashers, ...	·75	3 14 9	
Total, ...	7·91		111 19 6
In the ordinary service of the Prison.—			
Cleaning and jobbing work in and about the prison and prison yard and buildings (exclusive of building work of any kind), . .	6·77	76 0 1	
Cooking for the prisoners, . . .	7·60	63 19 7	
Keeping and attending sick prisoners, .	·15	1 4 7	
Pumping water for the service of the prison only.	3 47	20 5 7	
Repairing all kinds of prison clothing, .	1 90	16 16 6	
Repairing all kinds of prison shoes, . .	·74	11 6 3	
Making prison furniture, . . .	·36	8 16 9	
Total, ...	16·91		200 13 7
Non effective:—			
Sick, ...	1 91	—	
Under punishment, ...	·76	—	
Unemployed:—			
Awaiting trial, ...	5·57	—	
Debtors, ...	·93	—	
First-class misdemeanants, . . .	·17	—	
Others, &c., ...	9·61	—	
Total, ...	31·90	—	
Grand Total, ...	144 59	—	144 5 6

LIMERICK (FEMALE) PRISON.

Return by the Chief Warden, showing the employment of the Prisoners and value of their Earnings during the year ended 31st March, 1899.

Description of Employment.	Daily Average Number of Prisoners (for working days of the year.)	Value of Prisoners' Labour.	Total.
	F.	£ s. d.	£ s. d.
In Manufacture:—			
Knitting and needle working, . . .	2 68	50 0 0	
Washing, not including prisoners' clothing.	1 06	4 0 6	
Total, ...	3 90		54 5 6
In Buildings:—			
Painters and glaziers, ...	·16	4 16 6	
Whitewashers, ...	·16	5 15 9	
Total, ...	·30		8 16 5

LIMERICK (FEMALE) PRISON—*continued.*

Return by the CHIEF WARDER, showing the employment of the Prisoners and value of their Earnings during the year ended 31st March, 1899.

Description of Employment.	Daily Average Number of Prisoners (for the working days of the year).	Value of Prisoners' Labour.	Total.
	r.	£ s. d.	£ s. d.
In the ordinary service of the Prison:—			
Cleaning and jobbing work in and about the prison, and prison yard, and buildings (exclusive of building work of any kind),	4·40	43 0 5	
Cooking for the prisoners,	1·00	34 19 7	
Nursing prisoners' children,	2·70	—	
Repairing all kinds of prison clothing,	16·75	368 0 7	
Washing prisoners' clothing,	3·45	67 15 9	
Total,	27·90		404 16 4
Non-effective:—			
Sick,	1·04	—	
Under punishment,	·10	—	
Unemployed:—			
Awaiting trial,	1·77	—	
First-class misdemeanants,	1·20	—	
Others, &c.,	0·01	—	
Total,	0·00	—	
Grand Total,	41·11	—	587 17 4

LONDONDERRY PRISON.

Return by the GOVERNOR, showing the employment of the Prisoners and value of their Earnings during the year ended 31st March, 1899.

Description of Employment.	Daily Average Number of Prisoners (for working days of the year.)			Value of Prisoners' Labour.	Total.
	m.	r.	Total.	£ s. d.	£ s. d.
In Manufacture:—					
Knitting and woolworking,	—	14·	14·	162 33 7	
Matmaking, plaiting and other work connected therewith,	11·76	—	14 76	34 14 5	
Picking or teasing oakum, hair, &c.,	79·43	7·3	20·63	7 7 6	
Sackmaking,	6·15	1·77	6·93	14 19 3	
Stonebreaking,	9·11	—	9·44	3 8 1	
Washing and including prisoners' clothing,	—	·71	·71	5 3 7	
Woodcutting,	10·87	—	10·87	40 1 9	
Total,	61·7	17·41	67·71		591 3 7
In Buildings:—					
Bricklayers or masons,	·80	—	·80	1 13 0	
Carpenters or joiners,	·79	—	79	4 10 0	
Labourers,	0·	—	0·	40 0 0	
Painters and glaziers,	·50	—	·53	10 20 7	
Whitewashers,	·9	·07	·07	14 4 0	
Total,	0·5	·07	3·07		15 16 7

LONDONDERRY PRISON—*continued.*

Return by the Governor, showing the employment of the Prisoners and value of their Earnings during the year ended 31st March, 1899.

Description of Employment	Daily Average Number of Prisoners (for working days of the year.)			Value of Prisoners' Labour.	Total.
	M.	F.	Total.	£ s. d.	£ s. d.
In the ordinary service of the Prison : Cleaning and jobbing work in and about the prison and prison yard, and buildings (exclusive of building work of any kind),	137	79	16·6	137 7 9	
Cooking for the prisoners,	—	7	7	43 15 9	
Nursing and attending sick prisoners,	1·97	·46	2·18	44 0 9	
Repairing all kinds of prison clothing,	3·78	3·93	7·93	80 4 3	
Repairing all kinds of prison shoes,	98	—	·93	10 17 3	
Stoking prison furnaces,	·61	—	·61	4 16 6	
Washing prisoners' clothing,	—	4·93	4·93	48 4 3	
Gardening,	·15	—	·16	1 13 6	
Book-binding,	·19	—	·19	1 17 6	
Total,	10·76	17·71	28·40		484 1 5
Non-effectives:—					
Sick,	3·74	7·77	8·51	—	
Under punishment,	·19	·19	·77	—	
Unemployed :—					
Awaiting trial,	4·33	·33	8·54	—	
Debtors,	·17	—	·17	—	
First class misdemeanants,	·75	·1	·75	—	
Others, &c.,	3·61	6·79	9·7	—	
Total,	13·73	6·17	21·79	—	
Grand Total,	16·75	28·96	44·45	—	521 15 9

MOUNTJOY (MALE) PRISON.

Return by the Governor, showing the employment of the Prisoners and value of their Earnings during the year ended 31st March, 1899.

Description of Employment	Daily Average Number of Prisoners (for working days of the year.)	Value of Prisoners' Labour.	Total.
	M.	£ s. d.	£ s. d.
In Manufacture:—			
Brushmaking,	5·76	111 13 9	
Picking or teasing oakum, hair, &c.,	97·97	11 7 9	
Shoemaking,	20·61	64 15 9	
Sheemaking,	1·17	87 15 11	
Woodcutting,	33·17	163 5 4	
Mail bag making,	22·97	48 12 4	
Weaving frieze, &c.,	7·97	143 0 9	
Total,	186·90		133 12 0

MOUNTJOY (MALE) PRISON—*continued.*

Return by the GOVERNOR, showing the employment of the Prisoners and value of their Earnings during the year ended 31st March, 1899.

Description of Employment.	Daily Average Number of Prisoners (the working days of the year).	Value of Prisoners' Labour.	Total.
	M.	£ s. d.	£ s. d.
In Buildings :—			
Bricklayers or Masons.	72	6 6 5	
Carpenters or Joiners.	70	7 11 0	
Labourers,	5·68	34 9 5	
Painters and glaziers,	1·72	34 15 3	
Whitewashers,	·61	15 6 1	
Stonebreaking.	7·68	35 15 7	133 6 6
Total.	17·45		
In the ordinary service of the Prison :—			
Cleaning and jobbing work in and about the prison and prison yard and buildings (exclusive of building work of any kind).	19·14	729 18 5	
Nursing and attending sick prisoners,	1·97	23 6 6	
Repairing all kinds of prison clothing,	1·44	34 14 11	
Repairing all kinds of prison shoes,	·71	21 11 9	
Total.	18·75		816 10 6
Non-effective :—			
Sick,	16·75	—	
Under punishment,	·43	—	
Unemployed :—			
Debtors,	·74	—	
Others, &c.,	36·99	—	
Total.	43·73	—	
Grand Total,	78·74	—	1,171 7 6

MOUNTJOY (FEMALE) PRISON.

Return by the SUPERINTENDENT, showing the employment of the Prisoners and value of their Earnings during the year ended 31st March, 1899.

Description of Employment.	Daily Average Number of Prisoners (the working days of the year).	Value of Prisoners' Labour.	Total.
	F.	£ s. d.	£ s. d.
In Manufactures :—			
Knitting and needlework,	141·99	2,182 19 3	
Washing, not including prisoners' clothing.	34·15	828 6 6	3,011 5 9
Total.	180·64		
In the ordinary service of the prison :—			
Cleaning and jobbing work in and about the prison and prison yard, and building work (exclusive of building work of any kind).	11·97	169 12 9	
Repairing all kinds of prison clothing,	17·77	823 7 8	
Washing prisoners' clothing,	1·14	133 4 3	827 4 5
Total.	30·44		

MOUNTJOY (FEMALE) PRISON—*continued.*

Return by the Superintendent, showing the employment of the Prisoners and value of their Earnings during the year ended 31st March, 1899.

Description of Employment.	Daily Average Number of Prisoners (for working days of the year).	Value of Prisoners' Labour.	Total.
	v.	£ s. d.	£ s. d.
Non-effectives:—			
Sick,	·07	—	
Under punishment,	·11	—	
Unemployed:—			
Awaiting trial,	77·31	—	
Debtors,	·60	—	
First class misdemeanants,	·13	—	
Others, &c.,	13·13	—	
Total,	47·31	—	
Grand Total,	626·26	—	1,111 19 0

SLIGO PRISON.

Return by the Governor, showing the employment of the Prisoners and value of their Earnings during the year ended 31st March, 1899.

Description of Employment.	Daily Average Number of Prisoners (for working days of the year)			Value of Prisoners' Labour.	Total.
	m.	v.	Total.	£ s. d.	£ s. d.
In Manufactures:—					
Knitting and needleworking,	—	1·74	1·74	11 8 9	
Matmaking, plaiting, and other work connected therewith,	5·55	—	5·55	19 16 4	
Picking or teasing oakum, hair, &c.,	11·54	—	11·54	1 11 10	
Tinsmithing,	·45	—	·45	1 17 10	
Stoneworking,	14·41	—	14·44	6 19 0	
Washing, not knitting prisoners' clothing,	—	·1	·1	3 15 4	
Woodcutting,	5·37	—	3·83	61 8 9	
Total,	36·91	1·76	41·47		111 6 7
In Buildings:—					
Carpenters or joiners,	·45	—	·45	3 6 7	
Painters and glaziers,	·1	—	·1	10 3 3	
Plasterers,	·33	—	·43	17 19 4	
Whitewashers,	·19	—	·19	4 16 11	
Total,	1·14	—	1·10		34 14 9
In the ordinary service of the Prison:—					
Cleaning and jobbing work in and about the prison and prison yard and buildings (exclusive of building work of any kind),	6·06	·43	7·43	14 6 7	
Cooking for the prisoners,	1·ь	—	1·ь	51 10 7	
Nursing and attending sick prisoners,	·73	·43	·14	19 16 6	
Repairing all kinds of prison clothing,	1·73	6·41	6·19	109 13 9	
Repairing all kinds of prison shoes,	·73	—	·73	4 1 7	
Washing prisoners' clothing,	—	1·	1·	10 13 9	
Gardening,	1·97	—	1·97	51 9 8	
Total,	11·65	8·73	19·37		146 9 10

SLIGO PRISON—*continued.*

Return by the Governor, showing the employment of the Prisoners and value of their Earnings during the year ended 31st March, 1899.

Description of Employment.	Daily Average Number of Prisoners (for working days of the year).			Value of Prisoners' Labour.	Total.
	M.	F.	Total.	£ s. d.	£ s. d.
Non-effective:—					
Sick,	1·25	·38	1·87	—	
Under punishment,	·24	—	·24	—	
Unemployed:—					
Awaiting trial,	4·64	·43	5·07	—	
Debtors,	·93	—	·93	—	
First class misdemeanants,	·47	—	·47	—	
Others, &c.,	2·91	3·65	4·86	—	
Total,	9·35	5·90	15·25	—	
Grand Total,	57·65	16·87	74·48	—	444 1 2

TRALEE PRISON.

Return by the Governor, showing the employment of the Prisoners and value of their Earnings during the year ended 31st March, 1899.

Description of Employment.	Daily Average Number of Prisoners (for working days of the year).			Value of Prisoners' Labour.	Total.
	M.	F.	Total.	£ s. d.	£ s. d.
In Manufactures:—					
Making or teasing oakum, hair, &c.,	11·74	—	11·76	0 15 4	
Shoemaking,	·93	—	·93	6 6 5	
Stonebreaking,	13·25	—	13·25	67 14 10	
Washing, not including prisoners' clothing,	—	75	·75	2 17 10	
Woodmilling,	3·55	—	5·55	20 5 11	
Carpentry,	·93	—	·93	0 1 5	
Agriculture,	4·96	—	4·96	74 10 10	
Total,	27·93	75	35·25		156 11 7
In Buildings:—					
Bricklayers or masons,	·05	—	·05	0 13 3	
Carpenters or joiners,	·15	—	·15	1 10 0	
Labourers,	·53	—	·53	14 0 4	
Painters and glaziers,	·17	—	·17	5 1 5	
Smiths,	·93	—	·93	0 13 5	
Whitewashers,	·59	—	·59	10 0 5	
Total,	1·55	—	1·56		55 5 11
In the ordinary service of the Prison:—					
Cleaning and scrubbing work in and about the prison and prison yard and buildings (exclusive of building work of any kind),	5·75	·45	5·91	64 15 5	
Cooking for the prisoners,	—	1·	1·	31 19 7	
Nursing and attending sick prisoners,	·91	—	·91	6 4 6	
Repairing all kinds of prison clothing,	1·11	3·79	4·90	55 0 5	
Repairing all kinds of prison shoes,	·04	—	·09	1 11 5	
Washing prisoners' clothing,	—	1·23	1 23	70 20 5	
Total,	4 67	5·67	11·14		257 19 0

TRALEE PRISON—*continued.*

Return by the Governor, showing the employment of the Prisoners and value of their Earnings during the year ended 31st March, 1899.

Description of Employment.	Daily Average Number of Prisoners (for working days of the year).			Value of Prisoners' Labour.	Total.
	m.	f.	Total.	£ s. d.	£ s. d.
Non-effective :—					
Sick,	70	·6	·16	—	
Under punishment,	·84	·91	·36	—	
Unemployed :—					
Awaiting trial,	4·15	·10	1·89	—	
Debtors,	·43	·04	·47	—	
First class misdemeanants,	1·96	—	1·96	·—	
Others, &c.,	2·71	1·04	3·63	—	
Total,	9·16	1·61	10·77	—	
Grand Total,	47·27	9·65	56·85	—	409 16 4

TULLAMORE PRISON.

Return by the Governor, showing the employment of the Prisoners and value of their Earnings during the year ended 31st March, 1899.

Description of Employment.	Daily Average Number of Prisoners (for working days of the year).			Value of Prisoners' Labour.	Total.
	m.	f.	Total.	£ s. d.	£ s. d.
In Manufactures :—					
Picking or teasing oakum, hair, &c.,	7·90	—	7·90	0 12 0	
Sockmaking,	31·51	—	31·51	79 7 0	
Shoemaking,	·25	—	·25	0 1 4	
Tailoring,	·30	·60	1·00	1 8 11	
Washing, and [ ] prisoners' clothing	·—	1·50	1·50	1 15 5	... .
Woodworking,	·32	—	·32	0 9 7	
Total,	43·18	2·00	45·18		44 19 6
In Buildings :—					
Carpenters or joiners,	·91	—	·91	0 6 0	
Labourers,	3·68	—	3·43	29 3 4	
Painters and glaziers,	·72	—	·52	21 13 4	
Whitewashers,	·62	—	·42	12 9 4	
Total,	6·46	—	6·46		63 18 0
In the ordinary service of the Prison :—					
Cleaning and jobbing work in and about the prison and prison yard and buildings (exclusive of building work of any kind),	6·92	2·1	6·87	89 1 3	
Cooking for the prisoners,	7·—	—	7·—	69 10, 1·	
Nursing and attending sick prisoners,	·23	—	·36	1 8 4	
Repairing all kinds of prison clothing,	·62	9·01	9·23	97 14 6	
Repairing all kinds of prison shoes,	·—	·89	·89	1b 10 1	
Washing prisoners' clothing,	·34	1·55	1·90	99 17 0	
Total,	8·07	11·49	30·56		366 15 0

TULLAMORE PRISON—*continued.*

RETURN by the Governor, showing the employment of the Prisoners and value
of their Earnings during the year ended 31st March, 1899.

Description of Employment.	Daily Average Number of Prisoners (for working days of the year).			Value of Prisoners' Labour.	Total.
	m.	f.	Total.	£ s. d.	£ s. d.
Non-effective :—					
Sick, ...	1·20	·24	1·43	—	
Under punishment, ...	·42	·72	·64	—	
Unemployed :—					
Awaiting trial, ...	7·32	·42	7·73	—	
Debtors, ...	·94	—	·94	—	
First class misdemeanants, . .	2·15	—	2·15	—	
Others, &c., ...	2·41	1·95	3·43	—	
Total, ...	10·71	1·71	11·60	—	
Grand Total, . . .	24·13	16·23	41·44	—	444 0 4

WATERFORD PRISON.

RETURN by the Governor, showing the employment of the Prisoners and value
of their Earnings during the year ended 31st March, 1899.

Description of Employment.	Daily Average Number of Prisoners (for working days of the year).			Value of Prisoners' Labour.	Total.
	m.	f.	Total.	£ s. d.	£ s. d.
In Manufactures :—					
Knitting and needle working, . .	—	7·23	7·23	34 16 3	
Picking or teasing oakum, hair, &c.,	4·77	—	4·77	1 0 3	
Stone breaking, . . .	16·74	—	16·74	31 3 5	
Tailoring, ...	·7?	—	·7?	4 11 0	
Washing, and including prisoners' clothing,	—	4·77	4·7?	30 0 3	
Woodcutting, ...	11·40	—	11·40	33 11 11	
Total, . . .	37·70	9·90	13·70		106 15 1
In Buildings :—					
Bricklayers or Masons, . .	·74	—	·74	4 13 7	
Carpenters or Joiners, . .	·73	—	·73	4 14 . 0	
Labourers, ...	1·77	—	1·77	44 10 1	
Painters and Glaziers, . .	·9?	—	·9?	31 16 0	
Whitewashers, . . .	1·91	·41	1·42	40 10 1	
Total, ...	4·13	·41	4·70		123 1 5
In the ordinary service of the Prison :—					
Cleaning and jobbing work in and about the prison and prison yard and buildings (exclusive of building work of any kind), ...	4·73	7·40	7·91	132 14 4	
Cooking for the prisoners, . .	—	1·42	1·42	32 19 11	
Nursing and attending sick prisoners,	·74	1·14	1·74	41 18 3	
Pumping water for the service of the prison only, ...	1·44	—	1·14	40 4 0	
Repairing all kinds of prison clothing, .	4·73	4·44	7·13	121 13 11	
Stoking prison furnaces, . .	·41	—	·41	14 3 2	
Washing prisoners' clothing, . .	—	2·44	2·44	44 10 3	
Total, ...	4·79	16·23	24·14		417 4 10

110

Appendix to Twenty-first Report of the

WATERFORD PRISON—*continued.*

Return by the Governor, showing the employment of the Prisoners and value of their Earnings during the year ended 31st March, 1899.

Description of Employment.	Daily Average Number of Prisoners (for working days of the year).			Value of Prisoners' Labour.	Total.
	m.	f.	Total.	£ s. d.	£ s. d.
Non-effective :—					
Sick,	·74	·86	1·60	—	
Under punishment,	·15	·02	·17	—	
Unemployed :—					
Awaiting trial,	1·18	·01	1·19	—	
First class misdemeanants,	·94		·94	—	
Others, &c.,	1·94	1·17	3·11	—	
Total,	1·95	2·44	6·71	—	
Grand Total,	51·60	27·76	81·64	—	6·71 3 7

WEXFORD PRISON.

Return by the Governor, showing the employment of the Prisoners and value of their Earnings during the year ended 31st March, 1899.

Description of Employment.	Daily Average Number of Prisoners (for working days of the year).			Value of Prisoners' Labour.	Total.
	m.	f.	Total.	£ s. d.	£ s. d.
In Manufactures :—					
Mat-making, plaiting, and other work connected therewith,	3·72	—	3·72	16 5 1	
Picking or teasing oakum, hair, &c.	6·40	·01	6·44	20 19 0	
Shoemaking,	19·76	—	19·76	11 10 6	
Washing, not including prisoners' clothing,	—	·16	·16	6 13 4	
Woodcutting,	6·50	—	2·50	16 8 7	
Total,	27·50	·19	32·70		66 6 10
In Buildings :—					
Carpenters or joiners,	·16	—	·16	5 9 7	
Painters and glaziers,	·61	—	·61	13 13 1	
Smiths,	·61	—	·61	0 14 9	
Whitewashers,	·11	—	·11	6 6 3	
Total,	1·73	—	1·73		72 18 1
In the ordinary service of the Prison :—					
Cleaning and jobbing work in and about the prison and prison yard, and buildings (exclusive of building work of any kind),	8·77	·11	8·00	147 11 0	
Cooking for the prisoners,	·95	1·90	1·65	20 9 0	
Pumping water for the service of the prison only,	·61	—	·61	15 10 1	
Repairing all kinds of prison clothing,	·59	·71	6·61	70 3 11	
Repairing all kinds of prison shoes,	·16	—	·16	6 3 6	
Washing prisoners' clothing,	·37	·61	1·01	11 14 6	
Total,	10·64	6·97	16·90		962 4 9

WEXFORD PRISON.—*continued.*

Return by the Governor, showing the employment of the Prisoners and value of their Earnings during the year ended 31st March, 1899.

Description of Employment.	Daily Average Number of Prisoners (for working days of the year).			Value of Prisoners' Labour.	Total.
	m.	f.	Total.	£ s. d.	£ s. d.
Non-effective:—					
Sick,	·16	·01	·18	—	
Under punishment,	·19	—	·19	—	
Unemployed:—					
Awaiting trial,	1·09	·04	1·18	—	
Debtors,	·24	—	·21	—	
Others, &c.	3·18	·04	4·05	—	
Total,	5·78	·72	6·04	—	
Grand Total,				—	641 9 5

MINOR PRISONS.

CARRICK-ON-SHANNON PRISON.

Return by the Chief Warder, showing the employment of the Prisoners and value of their Earnings during the year ended 31st March, 1899.

Description of Employment.	Daily Average Number of Prisoners (for working days of the year)			Value of Prisoners' Labour.	Total.
	m.	f.	Total.	£ s. d.	£ s. d.
Non-remunerative:—					
Picking oakum,	·39	—	·39	—	
In Buildings:—					
Painters and glaziers,	·97	—	·97	2 19 8	
Whitewashers,	·10	—	·10	2 0 8	
Total,	·11	—	·37		4 12 4
In the ordinary service of the Prison:—					
Cleaning and jobbing work in and about the prison and prison yard, and buildings (exclusive of building work of any kind),	·15	·77	·92	19 0 0	
Pumping water for the service of the prison only,	·13	—	·13	2 0 6	
Repairing all kinds of prison clothing,	·04	·08	·12	3 0 7	
Washing prisoners' clothing,	—	·14	·14	6 7 4	
Total,	·64	·68	1 41		70 16 3
Unemployed:—					
Awaiting trial,	·85	·18	1 03	—	
Total,	·85	·18	1 03	—	
Grand Total,	2·56	·76	3·09	—	81 8 1

K

DROGHEDA PRISON.

Return by the Chief Warden, showing the employment of the Prisoners and value of their Earnings during the year ended 31st March, 1899.

Description of Employment.	Daily Average Number of Prisoners (for working days of the year).			Value of Prisoners' Labour.	Total.
	M.	F.	Total	£ s. d.	£ s. d.
In Manufacture:—					
Knitting and needleworking, . .	—	·07	·07	0 7 1	
Picking or teasing oakum, hair, &c.,	·23	—	·73	0 5 0	
Hemstreaking, ...	·99	—	·99	0 14 0	
Woodcutting, ...	·3]	—	·31	4 15 0	
Total, ...	1·23	·07	1·70		6 1 4
In Buildings:—					
Painters and glaziers, .	·03	—	·83	1 2 16	
Whitewashers, ...	·09	—	·09	7 16 6	
Total, . . .	·13	—	·13		8 13 10
In the ordinary service of the Prison :—					
Cleaning and jobbing work in and about the prison and prison yard, and buildings (exclusive of building work of any kind), ...	·74	·75	·97	18 18 0	
Cooking for the prisoners, . .	·47	·13	·13	74 0 0	
Nursing and attending sick prisoners, children, &c., ...	·36	·19	·74	4 5 0	
Repairing all kinds of prison clothing,	·01	·06	·07	1 17 0	
Washing prisoners' clothing, . .	—	·16	·14	0 1 3	
Total, ...	1·77	1·19	5·39		91 18 6
Non-effective :—					
Sick, ...	·04	·02	·06	—	
Under punishment, . . .	·91	—	·91	—	
Unemployed :—					
Awaiting trial, .	1·77	·16	1·65	—	
Total, . . .	1·73	·18	1·60	—	
Grand Total, . . .	6·34	1·37	6·71		91 6 0

ENNISKILLEN PRISON.

Return by the Chief Warden, showing the employment of the Prisoners and value of their Earnings, during the year ended 31st March, 1899.

Description of Employment.	Daily Average Number of Prisoners (for working days of the year).			Value of Prisoners' Labour.	Total.
	M.	F.	Total	£ s. d.	£ s. d.
Non-Remunerative, . . .	·04	—	·04	—	
In Manufacture :—					
Stoneworking, . . .	·99	—	·99	1 5 0	
Woodcutting, . . .	·31	—	·31	1 16 0	
Total, . . .	·41	—	·41		5 9 0
In Buildings :—					
Plasterers, ...	·04	—	·04	1 1 1	
Whitewashers, ...	·18	—	·19	4 17 7	
Total, . . .	·73	—	·73		5 15 0

ENNISKILLEN PRISON—*continued.*

RETURN by the CHIEF WARDER, showing the employment of the Prisoners and value of their Earnings during the year ended 31st March, 1899.

Description of Employment.	Daily Average Number of Prisoners (for working days of the year).			Value of Prisoners' Labour.	Total.
	M.	F.	Total.	£ s. d.	£ s. d.
In the ordinary service of the Prison :—					
Cleaning and jobbing work in and about the prison and prison yard, and buildings (exclusive of building work of any kind),	·46	·11	·55	7 16 6	
Nursing and attending sick prisoners,	·64	—	·64	0 13 8	
Repairing all kinds of prison clothing,	·53	·26	·56	0 13 0	
Washing prisoners' clothing,	·09	·12	·16	2 4 11	
Gardening,	·11	—	·13	1 10 11	
Total,	·46	·26	·92		13 1 10
Non-effective :—					
Sick,	·07	·13	·15	—	
Unemployed :—					
Awaiting trial,	·76	·06	·81	—	
Total,	·71	·07	·75	—	
Grand Total,	3·17	·56	3·56	—	31 17 6

MULLINGAR PRISON.

RETURN by the CHIEF WARDER, showing the employment of the Prisoners and value of their Earnings during the year ended 31st March, 1899.

Description of Employment.	Daily Average Number of Prisoners (for working days of the year).			Value of Prisoners' Labour.	Total.
	M.	F.	Total.	£ s. d.	£ s. d.
In Manufactures :—					
Picking or teasing oakum, hair, &c.,	—	·79	·79	—	
Shoemaking,	1·40	—	1·40	2 16 7	
Total,	1·19	·79	1·49		9 16 7
In Buildings :—					
Bricklayers or masons,	·01	—	·01	0 0 0	
Labourers,	·46	—	·46	1 16 0	
Painters and glaziers,	·03	—	·03	0 16 7	
Withdrawals,	·06	—	·06	1 0 3	
Total,	·16	—	·16		4 0 10
In the ordinary service of the Prison :—					
Cleaning and jobbing work in and about the prison and prison yard, and buildings (exclusive of building work of any kind),	·44	·17	·61	10 1 1	
Nursing and attending sick prisoners,	—	·01	·01	—	
Pumping water for the service of the prison only,	·72	—	·72	4 33 6	
Repairing all kinds of prison clothing,	·01	·31	·32	3 4 0	
Washing prisoners' clothing,	—	·18	·18	2 19 0	
Woodsplitting,	·11	—	·11	1 17 1	
Gardening,	·74	—	·74	4 8 3	
Total,	1·96	·67	1·70		27 1 0

MULLINGAR PRISON—*continued.*

Return by the Chief Warden, showing the employment of the Prisoners and value of their Earnings during the year ended 31st March, 1899.

Description of Employment.	Daily Average Number of Prisoners (for working days of the year)			Value of Prisoners' Labour.	Total.
	M.	F.	Total.	£ s. d.	£ s. d.
Non-effective:—					
Sick, ...	·01	·01	·02	—	
Unemployed:—					
Awaiting trial, . . .	·14	·59	73	—	
First class misdemeanants, : :	·01	—	·01	—	
Others, &c., ...	·01	·01	·02	· —	
Total, . . .	·17	·11	76	—	
Grand Total, . . .	1·98	1·91	6·96	—	14 6 3

OMAGH PRISON.

Return by the Chief Warden, showing the employment of the Prisoners and value of their Earnings during the year ended 31st March, 1899.

Description of Employment.	Daily Average Number of Prisoners (for working days of the year)			Value of Prisoners' Labour.	Total.
	M.	F.	Total.	£ s. d.	£ s. d.
In Manufactures:—					
Stonebreaking, . .	1·41	—	1·41	2 10 4	
Woodcutting, . . .	·07	—	·07	0 11 4	
Total, . . .	1·10	—	1·46		4 1 8
In Buildings:—					
Carpenters or joiners, . . .	·01	—	·01	0 16 0	
Labourers, . . .	·14	—	·11	3 15 0	
Painters and glaziers, . .	·11	—	·11	1 13 0	
Plasterers, . . .	·01	—	·01	0 16 0	
Smiths, . . .	·01	—	·01	0 11 0	
Whitewashers, . .	·11	—	·14	3 13 5	
Total, . . .	·41	—	·18		19 17 10
In the ordinary service of the Prison:—					
Cleaning and jobbing work in and about the prison and prison yard, and building (exclusive of building work of any kind), . . .	1·06	·18	1·21	25 16 0	
Nursing and attending sick prisoners, .	—	·14	·14	0 19 6	
Repairing all kinds of prison clothing, .	·04	·79	·43	9 1 4	
Washing prisoners' clothing, . .	—	·19	·19	5 16 0	
Total, . . .	1·10	·90	2·00		62 10 9
Non-effective:—					
Sick, ...	·06	—	·06	—	
Unemployed:—					
Awaiting trial, . . .	·79	·06	1·04	—	
Debtors, . . .	·04	—	·06	—	
Others, &c., . . .	·18	·03	76	—	
Total, . . .	1·77	·46	1·30	—	
Grand Total, . . .	6·72	·90	6·70	—	44 18 4

WICKLOW PRISON.

Return by the Chief Warder, showing the employment of the Prisoners and value of their Earnings during the year ended 31st March, 1899.

Description of Employment.	Daily Average Number of Prisoners (for working days of the year).			Value of Prisoners' Labour.	Total.
	M.	F.	Total.	£ s. d.	£ s. d.
In Manufacture:—					
Making or mending oakum, hair, &c.,	·71	—	·71	0 1 0	0 1 0
In Buildings:—					
Masons and glaziers, . . .	·04	—	·04	1 4 3	
Whitewashers, ...	·11	—	·11	2 16 7	
Total, ...	·15	—	·15		4 1 10
In the ordinary service of the Prison:—					
Cleaning and jobbing work in and about the prison and prison yard, and buildings (exclusive of building work of any kind), ...	·79	·01	·70	14 12 6	
Pumping water for the service of the prison only, ...	·42	—	·42	6 2 10	
Repairing all kinds of prison clothing,	·11	·03	·14	3 0 7	
Washing prisoners' clothing, . .	—	·07	·07	1 6 5	
Woodcutting, ...	·40	—	·43	0 12 1	
Total, ...	1·34	·16	1·52		27 17 5
Non-effective:—					
Sick, ...	·04	—	·04	—	
Under punishment, ...	·01	—	·01	—	
Unemployed:—					
Awaiting trial, ...	·41	·01	·42	—	
Others, &c., ...	·10	·04	·14	—	
Total, ...	·51	·05	·52	—	
Grand Total, ...	1·77	·73	1·60	—	32 0 3

RETURN showing the employment of Convicts and estimated
value of their Earnings

CORK MALE PRISON.

No. 1.—VALUE of the Labour of Convicts (as per measured work) for the
period from 1st April, 1898 to 12th June, 1898.

Work.	Daily Average (working days).	No. of Days.	Rate per day earned (see Summary).	Amount.
			d.	*£ s. d.*
Prison Buildings.	13·75	634	21 64	74 4 8
Prison Employment.	·23	2	16·	0 2 0
		636		74 6 8
Total,	13·99 × 50 =	634	21·75	74 6 8
		Working days.		

No. 2.—SUMMARY of Earnings of the various Trades or Parties for the period
from 1st April, 1898 to 12th June, 1898.

No. of Party.	Employment.	No. of Days.	Average Earnings per Convict per Day as measured and valued.	Amount.
			d.	*£ s. d.*
	PRISON EMPLOYMENT.			
—	Repairing prisoners' shoes,	2	15	0 2 0
	PRISON BUILDING.			
—	Bricklayers and Masons,	116	21·	11 10 0
—	Carpenters,	104	94·	35 0 0
—	Labourers,	268	16·	18 5 0
—	Smiths,	106	55·	19 16 0
	Total	634	21·61	74 4 0

RETURN showing the employment of Convicts and estimated
value of their Earnings—*continued.*

MARYBOROUGH CONVICT PRISON.

No. 1.—VALUE of Labour of Convicts (as per measured work) for the
year ended 31st March, 1899.

Work.	Daily Average (Working Days).	Number of Days.	Rate per day earned (per measure).	Amount.
			d.	£ s. d.
Prison Establishment.	39·700 / 41·965	18,423 / 18,442	—	18·71 / 18·76	437 9 1 / 360 4 5
Prison Employment,	39·? / 15·606	—	21,161 / 4,847	1·17? / 1?	1,406 17 9 / 218 7 0
Totals,	94·6	—	29,831	1·16	1,742 1 9
NON-EFFECTIVE.				
Under Punishment, &c., Excused from Labour on Medical grounds.	·185 / 6·577	—	160 / 1,992	—	
Grand Totals,	103·673 × 303 =	—	31,171	13·53	1,749 4 9

No. 2.—SUMMARY of Earnings of the various Trades or Parties, for the year
ended 31st March, 1899.

No. of Party.	Employment.	No. of Days.	Average Earnings per Convict per Day as measured and valued.	Amount.
	MANUFACTORY.		d.	£ s. d.
—	Tailoring,	1,363	1?	83 16 11
—	Shoemaking,	530	1?	35 3 2
—	Labouring on Prison Farm,	16,111	15	416 11 6
		18,039	18·71	437 9 1
	PRISON BUILDINGS.			
—	Carpenters,	576	21	47 12 0
—	Smithing,	303	24	20 4 6
—	Labourers,	11,713	16	751 16 6
		12,463	10·75	646 8 6
	PRISON EMPLOYMENT.			
—	Labourers,	144	18	81 9 6
—	Cleaning Prison,	9,837	17	141 16 6
—	Repairing Clothing and Bedding,	737	18	11 18 6
—	Washing Clothing and Bedding,	806	17	46 9 6
—	Cooking,	999	15	42 9 6
	—	4,847	18	1?? 7 6

RETURN showing the employment of Convicts and estimated
value of their Earnings—*continued.*

MOUNTJOY CONVICT PRISON.

No. I.—VALUE of the Labour of Convicts (as per measured work), for the
year ended 31st March, 1899.

Work.	Daily Average (working days.)	No. of Days.	Rate per day earned here (Summary).	Amount.
Manufactory,	14591½	12,691·761	—	1·77	2,2¢4 16 ¢
Prison Buildings,	28118	7,587·148 44,396·619	1975	491 10 11
Prison Employment,	89·981	—	6,332·097	14 11	9,204 7
Totals,	107·707	44,742·831	13·45	4,100 12 9
NON-EFFECTIVE.				
Sick,	19·570	5,794·373	—	—
Punishment,	7.14	737 920	—	—
Not told off to parties,	1·948	441,130	4,049·146	—
		Working days.		
Grand Totals,	749·800 × 143 =	61,493·177	13·11	3,160 19 9

No. 2.—SUMMARY of the Earnings of the various Trades or Parties, for the
year ended 31st March, 1899

No. of Party.	Employment.	No. of Days.	Average Earnings per Convict per Day as measured and valued.	Amount.
	MANUFACTORY.		d.	£ s. d.
—	Tailoring,	17,845 747	1·92	1,249 0 1
—	Shoemaking,	10,148 838	1·63	910 0 6
—	Matmaking,	8,819·315	1·76	48 1 5
—	Mail Bag Making,	845·188	·7	9 1 1
—	Oakum Picking,	2,077 947	·1	9 17 1
—	Tinsmithing,	307·894	34·	88 4 9
—	Carpentering,	488·	16·2	42 0 8
—	Baking,	1,707 647	1·2	319 3 7
		42,691·751	1·77	2,204 16 6
	PRISON BUILDINGS.			
—	Labouring,	5,177 964	16·	727 17 6
—	Hem+king,	458 448	21·	55 7 7
—	Carpentering,	2,344 591	24·	214 11 0
—	Painting,	600·118	70·8	42 0 11
—	Whitewashing,	91·438	17·	4 11 6
		7,307·148	1675	491 10 11
	PRISON EMPLOYMENT.			
—	Cleaning,	2,847 747	19·	191 11 9
—	Store Porters,	189·991	13·	45 5 1
—	Stokers,	141 561	10·	9 15 9
—	Cooks,	2,189 971	18·4	167 17 7
—	Bookbinding,	196·161	94·	16 10 3
—	Nursing,	199 014	19 8	9 9 6
		6,332·097	16·51	945 8 4

RETURN showing the employment of Convicts and estimated
value of their Earnings—*continued.*

MOUNTJOY FEMALE CONVICT PRISON.

No. 1.—VALUE of the Labour of Convicts (as per measured work) for the
year ended 31st March, 1899.

Work.	Daily Average (working days).	No. of Days.	Rate per day earned (see Summary).	Amount.
			d.	*£ s. d.*
Manufactory,	13·51	4,093·93	10·	170 11 3
Prison employment,	8·1	2,007·49	11·05	147 9 9
Totals,	20·54	—	6,161·97	12·36	817 17 0
NON-EFFECTIVE.				
Punishment,	·85	709	—	—
Sick in Cells, &c. ,	·61	801·91	—	—
Hospital, ,	5·10	1,030·70	1,572·70	—	—
		Working days.		Average earnings.
				d.
Grand Totals,	84·51	X 803 =	7,445·93	10·91	811 11 0

No. 2.—SUMMARY of Earnings of the various Trades or Parties, for the
year ended 31st March, 1899.

No. of Party.	Employment.	No. of Days.	Average Earnings per Convict per day as measured and valued.	Amount.
	MANUFACTORY.		*d.*	*£ s. d.*
—	Knitting and Needlework, ,	4,092·13	10·	170 11 8
	PRISON EMPLOYMENT.			
—	Cooking for the Prisoners,	1,054·74	23·	101 14 1
—	Cleaning Prison, , ,	941·75	10·3	19 1 8
		7,007·49	11·05	117 9 9

Daily Average Number of Convicts in Custody during the Year, . . 74·51
Percentage on Prison Population Working, ... 87·4
Do. do. do. Sick, &c., ... 11·3
Do. do. do. in Punishment, ... ·19

Table XXV.—Number Sentenced to Police Supervision, and Number Discharged under Police Supervision, &c., for each Year from 1870.

TABLE XXVI.—NUMBER of habitual criminals and discharged convicts registered in :

Year.	No.	Year	No.
1870,	907	1885–86,	202
1871,	7,058	1886–87,	950
1872,	840	1887–88,	155
1873,	1,118	1888–89,	160
1874,	1,062	1889–90,	131
1875,	985	1890–91,	133
1876,	964	1891–92,	144
1877,	679	1892–93,	140
1878,	272	1893–94,	126
1879,	306	1894–95,	161
1880–81*,	265	1895,	159
1881–82,	224	1896,	167
1882–83,	189	1897,	174
1883–84,	164	1898,	156
1884–85,	172		

* From 1st January, 1880, to 31st March, 1881.

TABLE XXVII.—Return showing the Expenditure
and Mainten

HEADS OF SERVICE.	Totals.
Daily average number of prisoners (including Minor Prisons and Bridewells).	{MALES, 2,261} {FEMALES, 618} Total, 2,979
A.—COST OF STAFF.	£ s. d.
Pay and allowance of officers, including uniforms, &c., and fine fund.	49,766 0 3
Average annual charge per prisoner,	16 11 9
B.—MAINTENANCE OF PRISONERS.	
Victualling for prisoners,	21,162 13 1
Medicines, surgical instruments, &c.	475 6 9
Fuel, light, and water,	5,303 16 2
Soap, scouring and cleaning articles,	601 16 0
Clothing for prisoners,	2,669 17 6
Bedding for prisoners,	311 17 8
Furniture, kitchen utensils, crockery, &c.	167 16 6
Total expenses of Maintenance,	29,591 0 2
Average annual charge per prisoner,	10 4 1

HEADS OF SERVICE.	Armagh.	Belfast.
Daily average number of prisoners (including Minor Prisons and Bridewells).	{m. 66} {f. 17}	m. 838 f. 114
A.—COST OF STAFF.	£ s. d.	£ s. d.
Pay and allowances of officers, including uniforms, &c., and fine fund.	1,746 19 6	4,317 10 1
Average annual charge per prisoner,	21 4 7	9 6 6
B.—MAINTENANCE OF PRISONERS.		
Victualling for prisoners,	697 16 1	2,563 6 6
Medicines, surgical instruments, &c.,	77 11 9	66 19 6
Fuel, light, and water,	200 8 1	666 6 6
Soap, scouring and cleaning articles,	26 15 10	66 13 0
Clothing for prisoners,	76 16 7	666 10 6
Bedding for prisoners,	16 2 6	66 6 6
Furniture, kitchen utensils, crockery, &c.,	13 16 3	66 7 6
Total expenses of Maintenance,	997 3 1	3,656 6 6
Average annual charge per prisoner,	12 0 8	7 16 0

and Local Prison (including Minor Prisons and Bridewells) for Staff ended 31st March, 1899.

Maryborough.		HEADS OF SERVICE.
N. 164	—	Daily average number of prisoners (including Minor Prisons and Bridewells).
		A.—COST OF STAFF.
£ s. d. 3,163 3 7	£ s. d. —	Pay and allowances of officers, including uniforms, &c., and fire fund.
64 3 6	—	Average annual charge per prisoner.
		B.—MAINTENANCE OF PRISONERS.
1,630 0 7	—	Victualling for prisoners.
67 0 3	—	Medicines, surgical instruments, &c.
375 0 7	—	Fuel, light, and water.
30 16 10	—	Soap, scouring and cleaning articles.
817 11 11	—	Clothing for prisoners.
57 16 4	—	Bedding for prisoners.

A. COST OF STAFF.

	£	s.	d.
Pay and allowances of officers, including uniforms, &c., and gas fund	1,375	1	0
Average annual charge per prisoner, ...	17	0	7

B.—MAINTENANCE OF PRISONERS.

	£	s.	d.
Victualling for prisoners, ...	412	0	0
Medicines, surgical instruments, &c.	16	0	0
Fuel, light, and water, ...	794	10	0
Soap scouring and cleaning articles, ...	15	0	0
Clothing for prisoners, ...	43	11	0
Bedding for prisoners, ...	9	17	2
Furniture, kitchen utensils, crockery, &c., . . .	71	10	3

and Local Prison (including Minor Prisons and Bridewells) for Staff
ended 31st March, 1899—*continued.*

Kilmainham.	Limerick, Male.	Limerick, Female.	Londonderry.	HEADS OF SERVICE.
D. 155	D. 104	F. 41	{ M. 115½ F. 41½ }	Daily average number of prisoners (including Minor Prisons and Bridewells).
				A.—COST OF STAFF.
£ s. d. 2,619 17 1	£ s. d. 3,061 0 0	£ s. d. 179 0 0	£ s. d. 2,351 1 0	Pay and allowances of officers, including uniforms, &c., and fine fund.
16 9 6	19 17 6	17 15 7	16 7 10	Average annual charge per prisoner.
				B.—MAINTENANCE OF PRISONERS.
776 5 9	574 9 5	0 6	5 a 49 3	Victualling for prisoners.
18 11 6	7 16 6	6 6 11	11 16 8	Medicines, surgical instruments, &c.
195 10 6	205 15 11	165 15 10	627 11 10	Fuel, light, and water.
82 21 7	51 17 7	19 1 6	36 11 0	Soap, scouring and cleaning articles.
130 18 5	94 1 7	25 5 6	179 11 10	Clothing for prisoners.
17 5 7	16 19 6	5 4 0	37 15 5	Bedding for prisoners.
17 4 2	18 6 5	11 15 5	73 7 6	Furniture, kitchen utensils, crockery, &c.
1,534 8 10	945 9 4	455 19 6	1,612 10 9	Total expenses of Maintenance.

TABLE XXVII.—(*continued*)—C. Expenses of Convict and Local Prisons, other than for Staff and Maintenance, in the year ended 31st March, 1899.

HEADS OF SERVICE.	TOTALS.
	£ s. d.
Gratuities to prisoners (including grant to Discharged Prisoners' Aid Society),	957 1 2
Escort and conveyance of prisoners,	3,575 10 1
New buildings and alterations,	6,934 13 6
Ordinary repairs of buildings,	3,052 10 11
Rent,	504 17 1
Incidental expenses (including travelling and general expenses of officers),	1,723 9 1
Maintenance of children of female prisoners,	7 0 7
Washing for public departments,	—
Total of other expenses,	20,755 5 5
Do. exclusive of New buildings and alterations and Washing for public departments,	16,759 9 11
Average annual charge per prisoner,	6 7 10

SUMMARY OF A, B, AND C.

	£ s. d.
A.—Total cost of Staff,	49,755 9 5
B.— „ Maintenance,	29,621 0 9
C.— „ Other expenses (exclusive of New buildings, &c. and Washing for public departments),	16,759 9 11
Total expenses for the year,	96,136 9 6
Total annual charge per prisoner,	37 11 5
DEDUCTIONS:	
Appropriations in aid, viz.:—Net receipts on Manufacturing department; and Miscellaneous receipts from sale of old stores, rents, &c.,	4,754 11 6
Net cost (after above deduction),	91,161 18 0
Net annual charge per prisoner (after above deduction),	31 9 6

Note.—No deduction is made in respect of the labour of prisoners employed on prison buildings or in prison manufactories, but the value of such labour in the year 1898-99 is calculated at £16,444 12s. 3d.

TABLE XXVIII.—STATEMENT of Expenses of Convict and Local Prisons in each year, from 1892–93 to 1898–99.

HEADS OF SERVICE	Year, 1892–93. Prisoners: Male, 2,176. Female, 288.	Year, 1893–94. Prisoners: Male, 1,985. Female, 473.	Year, 1894–95. Prisoners: Male, 2,130. Female, 433.	Year, 1895–96. Prisoners: Male, 1,988. Female, 433.	Year, 1896–97. Prisoners: Male, 1,710. Female, 257.	Year, 1897–98. Prisoners: Male, 1,108. Female, 2,701.	Year, 1898–99. Prisoners: Male, 2,230. Female, 200.
Pay and allowances of officers, including uniforms, &c.							
Victualling for prisoners,							
Clothing for prisoners,							
Bedding for prisoners,							
Furniture, kitchen utensils crockery, &c.							
Medicines, surgical instruments, &c.							
Gratuities to prisoners (including Grant to Discharged Prisoners' Aid Society),							
Fuel, light, and water,							
Soap, scouring and cleaning articles,							
Rent,							
Rates and conveyance of prisoners,							
New buildings and alterations,							
Ordinary repairs of buildings,							
Incidental Expenses,							
Maintenance of children of female prisoners,							
Washing for public departments,							
Totals, exclusive of New buildings and alterations, and Washing for public departments,							

DUBLIN : Printed for Her Majesty's Stationery Office
By ALEX. THOM & CO. (Limited), 87, 88, & 89 Abbey-street.
The Queen's Printing Office.